**DEBRETT'S**

LONDON 1769

OF MODERN MANNERS

**Debrett's A–Z of Modern Manners**
Published by Debrett's Limited
www.debretts.com

Original 2008 edition by Elizabeth Wyse, Jo Bryant, Sarah
Corney and Ruth Massey, with special articles by Susannah Jowitt

Revisions and updates: Lucy Hume

Consulting editor: Renée Kuo

Designer: Renata Masini

ISBN 978-1-9997670-2-0

Printed and bound by L.E.G.O. Group, Italy

*'What do you think of modern civilisation?'*
*'I think it would be a good idea.'*

MAHATMA GANDHI

AEROPLANES TO
AWAKE, STAYING

## AEROPLANES

In cramped conditions, 35,000 feet above sea level, good manners are more important than ever, so follow a few guidelines for civilised air travel:

- Avoid encroaching on other passengers' territory by keeping your elbows to yourself and bags stowed away.
- It shouldn't be necessary to recline your seat on a short flight, but if you do need to do so, ease it down gently to avoid crushing the legs of the passenger behind.
- If you have children, ensure that they do not kick or fiddle with the seat in front. However innocent and playful their behaviour, it's considerably less adorable to others than it is to you.
- If the passenger next to you is holding a baby, smile and deploy all your reserves of patience. Flying can be traumatic for infants and young children so however piercing their screams, don't let your displeasure show.
- Drink in moderation. You might be the life of the party after a tipple, but no one will appreciate your drunken antics in an enclosed space.
- Think twice before initiating a conversation with your neighbours, particularly if they are wearing headphones or engrossed in a book.
- If you do get chatting, choose your topics wisely. Many people are terrified of flying, and will not take kindly to jokes about turbulence, terrorists or the competence of the flight crew.

• Stay relaxed when embarking or disembarking and
don't barge your way to the exit. Help others to stow
(or remove) luggage in the overhead lockers if
necessary. Behave courteously towards the flight crew
and be sure to thank them for their service.

### AFFECTION, PUBLIC DISPLAYS OF

Overly amorous public displays are embarrassing for
those forced to witness private moments. Holding hands,
being close and quick kisses are acceptable, but excessive
physical intimacies should be reserved for the bedroom.

### AFTERSHAVE

Use aftershave discriminately: people don't want to be
able to smell you before they see you.

### AGE

While children are usually proud to get older, for the
rest of us, each new birthday can become an
increasingly daunting prospect.

It's rude to ask someone their age, and trying to
guess is ill-advised (if you do, make sure you subtract
a decade or two).

If someone does ask you your age, don't be tempted
to lie: whatever the number, be proud of it. With age

comes experience, wisdom, contentment – even prosperity, if you're lucky.

## ALLERGIES

Allergies can range from the life-threatening to the merely unconfortable, but should be taken seriously however severe they are.

If you have an allergy, clearly inform your host in advance of any occasion at which food will be served.

As a host, take this information into account when planning your menu, but try to avoid making the allergy-sufferer feel singled out or short-changed – serving them a bed of lettuce when everyone else is tucking in to Beef Wellington might leave them feeling like a culinary pariah.

In certain circumstances (a large catered wedding breakfast, for example), it can be helpful to offer to bring your own packed lunch or supper if you suffer from an allergy.

*See also: Intolerances, Food*

## ANGER

*'Anger fed is dead – 'Tis starving makes it fat.'*
EMILY DICKINSON

In the coolly reserved climate of modern UK society, anger is often seen as socially unacceptable, but don't

underestimate its ability to clear the air. Sulking does not accomplish this, leaving rage to fester and intensify.

Losing your temper can have consequences, however, so be prepared to pay the price for words discharged in anger. The joy of fury is one-sided: you may thrill to the rush of blood to the head, the excitement of finally being brave enough to say what you want, but the other person will just see a lunatic spewing insults.

So enjoy anger, but use it wisely — it can rebound on its perpetrator. Employ devastating logic rather than insults, even when your ire is at its peak. If the tables are turned and the anger is directed at you, just laugh — there is no better way of deflating someone else's balloon of hot air.

### APOLOGISING

The British have a reputation for near-compulsive apologising: the reflexive 'sorry' when someone else barges into you, the 'apologies for clogging up your inbox' at the start of an e-mail.

Constant, needless apologising devalues the currency and will lessen the impact of a genuine, heartfelt *mea culpa*.

A sincere apology should always be offered when your actions have had a negative impact on other people, however. Even if you don't fully understand why someone is upset, respect their feelings and accept that your actions are the cause. Don't pass the buck or use your apology as a way of blaming someone else (a 'nonpology').

An apology will be much more persuasive if you acknowledge the fault: 'I'm sorry I was so late' is more specific than a simple 'I'm sorry', and actually recognises the other person's grievance.

If you have committed a real faux pas, consider sending a handwritten note — but only after you have offered a verbal apology, otherwise it will look like cowardice.

If you are offered a genuine apology, acknowledge it graciously and move on without trying to elicit grovelling self-abasement.

## APPLAUSE

Hand-clapping is the usual way of demonstrating approval or recognising achievement. Cheering, whooping, whistling and standing ovations are also increasingly used to convey appreciation: traditional British reserve is often abandoned in the communal euphoria that greets an impressive performance.

A slow handclap, conversely, signals discontent from an audience that has been kept waiting. Booing a performer is never acceptable.

At the opera, applaud after the overture (before curtain-up), after an impressive aria (but never while someone is singing), at the end of a scene or act and, of course, at the end of the production. It is also the norm to clap the conductor when he or she takes to the podium before the performance, after the interval and at the end

(when the orchestra also takes a bow).

At seated musical concerts, it is customary to applaud between different compositions, but not between movements within a piece.

At the theatre, applause is expected at the end of each act, after a notable scene or moment ('A handbag?!') and at the end of a production.

## ARGUMENTS

*'Arguments are to be avoided: they are always vulgar and often convincing.'*
OSCAR WILDE

An argument can be both electrifying and exciting, but often the most satisfying ones do not descend into anger, remaining untainted by the red mist of rage. After all, the 'aim' of an argument should not be solely to win, but to progress the basic understanding of the issue at hand – and this is achieved more easily if everyone remains calm.

Arguing in person will always be more rewarding than bickering via text message or email – nuance and meaning can be lost in writing, which is frustrating when you're trying to make a point.

Being the more civil person will ensure that you retain the moral high ground. You shouldn't need to shout to make your point. Stick to arguing about facts, not the personalities of the people with whom you're arguing.

Concede a point when you have no response to it, and

if your argument is based on bias or intuition alone, have the honesty to admit it — this arms you with a reputation for being reasonable, which confers more power than just ranting. Apologise on the spot if you've said something you might regret later.

Underlying all the disagreement is an agreement that the other person's opinion is valid, and that you are at least going to listen to it. It's not worth the effort of arguing with anyone who doesn't listen to your point of view — or simply talks over you.

## ART GALLERIES

Art galleries tend to be hushed, peaceful places, so respect this environment by keeping your voice low and switching your phone to silent. Don't stand in front of the paintings for a long time, or barge in front of other people, and comply with any rules on taking photographs.

Wear any specialist knowledge lightly, and don't lecture others. It's not necessary to like or understand everything, but keep strong opinions to yourself ('Call that art?' or 'My two-year-old does better!').

## AVOCADOS

The photogenic avocado has become a brunch-time favourite, with worldwide production doubling over the last 15 years to cater for the spike in demand.

Its health benefits may have been over-hyped, but an avocado is still better for you than a chocolate bar – low in sugar, it contains healthy fats and lots of vitamins.

Whether you're preparing it smashed, sliced or whole with an egg baked into the central well, make sure you don't become a victim of 'avocado hand' – the injury caused by accidentally cutting yourself when trying to extract the slippery stone. Aficionados recommend scooping it out with a spoon instead, or placing the centre of the blade into the stone, then twisting.

*See also: Millennials*

## AWAKE, STAYING

*'Sleeping is no mean art: for its sake one must stay awake all day.'*
FRIEDRICH NIETZSCHE

We've all been there: in the warm, dark intimacy of the theatre, you've fallen asleep before the end of the first act. Then there's the head-nodding on the train, the snoring during the spa treatment, the dinner party where you feel your eyes rolling up into your head, even as you glimpse the horrified expression of the person talking to you.

We live fast-paced, frenetic lives, and inadvertent daytime micro-naps are a sign of our systems trying to catch up.

Going to bed earlier and getting up earlier will help you feel more rested and lively, but this can be hard to achieve. Avoid the jolt-crash cycle of caffeine and sugary snacks, and choose instead herbal teas and slow-release foods like oatcakes or bananas.

Alternatively, you can give up the battle and become comfortable with your cat-napping: warn people to pinch you in theatres, ask someone to wake you before your stop on train journeys. If you *do* fall asleep in a social context, apologise profusely, explain why you are exhausted (insomnia, jet lag, overwork), make your excuses and go home to bed.

*See also: Zzzzz*

BABIES TO
BUSINESS TRIPS

## BABIES

New parents may need to rein in their enthusiasm for their bundle of joy: it is unrealistic to expect your friends to be as happy and proud as you.

Similarly, baby photos will have limited appeal for others, and video footage should be reserved for members of your close family.

The precise timing of tooth-cutting, first word, first solid food and first steps are details that only you and your health professional need to know. Don't imagine that it's suddenly acceptable to rhapsodise on the contents of your child's nappies, or to ignore its screams.

If you're presented with a baby, be sure to coo with untrammelled enthusiasm. Understand that parents may be exhausted and frazzled, and may not take kindly to advice, however well-intended.

*See also Aeroplanes; Children*

## BAD NEWS

Being the bearer of bad news is an unenviable job — and one where the gravity of the task often drives rationality out of the window.

Whether the news is of bereavement or redundancy, it should be imparted in person wherever possible. Establish eye contact and have tissues ready. If you know the other person well, a physical gesture, such as putting an arm around their shoulder, may be appropriate.

Speak slowly and clearly, leaving no room for uncertainty (which could lead to misleading hope) and pre-empting as many of their questions as possible, so that they don't have to pull themselves together to speak. Choose the place in which you deliver the news sensibly – make sure you will be uninterrupted, that your mobile is switched off and that you can give the receiver your undivided attention.

Don't feel you have to offer words of comfort, and don't try to make light of the situation. Your role as the bad-news-giver is to make the communication as pain-free as possible, but not to mitigate the news itself.

If you're giving news of a death or serious illness, make sure the other person knows that you're going to be there for them as long as they need.

## BALDNESS

Take inspiration from bald icons like Stanley Tucci, Bruce Willis and Jason Statham and accept your thinning hair by keeping it very short or shaved.

Be grateful for the money you're saving on expensive hair products, be sure to wear sun cream in warm weather, and never be tempted to sport a comb-over.

## BAR MITZVAHS AND BAT MITZVAHS

Bar Mitzvahs and Bat Mitzvahs are Jewish coming-of-age

ceremonies, held when a boy turns 13 (a Bar Mitzvah) and when a girl turns 12 (a Bat Mitzvah). They are the most important rites of passage in the Jewish faith.

The rites and rituals of Bar and Bat Mitzvahs can vary widely depending on the congregation, and a service can last between one-and-a-half and three hours.

Formal invitations are sent out by the parents, inviting guests to the ceremony at the synagogue, and to attend the reception afterwards at their home/venue, which can range from a festive meal to a lavish party. Guests should respond with a handwritten reply. For less formal celebrations, invitations are often a note or postcard, email, or by word of mouth – in which case respond in kind.

Presents are given by guests but, as with a wedding, are either sent in advance or taken to the post-ceremony celebrations – not to the synagogue.

Guests should arrive at the synagogue on foot (devout Jews do not drive during the day on Saturdays) and dress appropriately. Men should wear a formal suit and skullcap (which are often handed out at the synagogue for Gentiles), women smart day dress (ensuring their arms are covered above the elbow and their legs above the knee) and a hat.

Men and women will often be seated separately. While there is usually singing during the ceremony, some of the service may involve standing in silence. Appropriate times to leave the room may be observed from the actions of the congregation. Keep your mobile phone turned off — Orthodox Jews do not use electrical devices on Saturdays.


## BARBECUES

Preparation is everything when you're hosting a barbecue. Ensure that the barbecue is lit and ready before guests arrive so that they're not waiting around feeling famished while you try to locate the matches.

Provide enough comfortable seats for all the guests — they won't be able to enjoy themselves as much if they're having to juggle food and drink. Make sure there is plenty of shade; if you are fortunate enough to have good weather, the sun may be hazardous. Provide plenty of water; it will keep your guests hydrated, and may prolong the supply of chilled beer and wine. Similarly, have a wet-weather plan and indoor seating in case of showers.

Be aware of your neighbours and try to position the barbecue so that smoke doesn't drift into other people's gardens. (Better still, pre-empt the problem altogether by inviting them.)

Barbecuing can bring out a chef's baser tendencies towards one-upmanship, but competition over marinade ingredients and grilling techniques should only ever be initiated with tongue firmly in cheek. Make sure you prepare a vegetarian option for those who don't eat meat.

## BARS

At a crowded bar, respect the 'first-come, first-served' rule. Make eye contact with the bartender, and remain patient if you are not served immediately. Don't wave a note, click your fingers or shout to get attention: you'll only persuade the bar staff to ignore you.

If you're unsure whether it's your turn, look around and gesture 'after you' to anyone looking expectant.

Don't intrude on others' evenings with rowdy drinking games or overly-loud conversations. If you accidentally jostle someone and spill their drink, offer to replace it.

Always tip the staff in a bar with table service. This is generally 12.5 per cent and may be added to the bill, but leave cash, or add it on to your final payment, if not.
*See also Pubs*

## BEACHES

The beach is an unusual public area where we strip down to the equivalent of our knickers. However, even in such relaxed surroundings, behaviour should be governed by consideration for others.

Respect other people's space, staying at least a towel's width away from the next encampment, and keep any dogs and children under control. Take any rubbish with you when you leave.

Shake towels out with full consideration of the wind

direction. Music should only be played through headphones, never speakers. Team sports should be reserved for quiet, unpopulated stretches of sand. Respect the coastguard and take note of any signs or flags.

It goes without saying that you shouldn't ogle other sunbathers – and don't think that hiding behind sunglasses makes it OK. Cover up when not on the beach with a tunic, sarong or t-shirt. Don't forget the sun cream and, if appropriate, offer to help your companions with any hard-to-reach spots.

## BEARDS

*'How many cowards wear yet upon their chins the beards of Hercules and frowning Mars!'*
WILLIAM SHAKESPEARE

Beards have enjoyed a renaissance over the last few years, but has their ubiquity meant we've reached 'peak beard'?

Whatever their fashion credentials, beards should be kept clean and in shape. Wash, shampoo and trim regularly. Watch out for froth (cappuccino, Guinness) and sauces (ketchup, mayonnaise).

Comedy beards and goatees are to be avoided once you've left your student days behind you.
*See also Stubble*

## BILL, PAYING THE

Whoever has issued an invitation – whether it's to lunch, dinner or drinks – should usually pay. Business lunches aside, however, life isn't simple, and dating even less so. All too often, the arrival of the bill brings with it an unwelcome awkwardness and a second-guessing of expectations.

Going Dutch is an option, and it's customary to split the bill for larger group meals, but it can seem a too-clinical transaction in the context of a romantic encounter. Alternatively, you could both insist on paying until one of you eventually concedes and promises to make up for it next time.

If your date just involves drinks, it's perfectly acceptable for you each to buy alternate rounds.
*See also Going Dutch; Restaurants*

## BIRTH ANNOUNCEMENTS

All family members and close friends should be phoned soon after a birth and told the good news. This is traditionally the responsibility of the father.

It's fine to let others know by text message, email or through social media, but be careful that the news doesn't leak out before those closest to you have been told.

Birth announcement cards, if used, should read:
*James and Anna Robinson are happy to announce the birth of their son, Thomas Charles*

The baby's date of birth and weight are included and a pink or blue ribbon may be attached.

A short birth announcement can also be placed in a local or national newspaper if desired, for example:

*Robinson — On 20th February to James and Anna, a son, Thomas Charles*

If the parents do not share the same surname, both surnames should be included:

*Carter Jones — On 20th February to Andrew Carter and Jeremy Jones, a son, Oliver Theodore*

In the case of a single parent:

*Lamont — On 20th February to Leila, a daughter, Natalie Emma*

## BLACK TIE

If required, black tie (sometimes referred to as 'dinner jacket' or in America as 'tuxedo'), will be specified on invitations. Traditional black tie consists of:

- Black wool dinner jacket. Single-breasted with no vents, silk peaked lapels (or a shawl collar) and covered buttons.
- Black trousers — slightly tapered — with a single row of braid down each outside leg.
- White marcella evening shirt with a soft turn-down collar, worn with cufflinks and studs.

- A black bow tie, which must be hand tied; avoid novelty ties or colours.

  Highly polished or patent black lace-up shoes and black silk socks.

  A white silk scarf is an optional accessory. Cummerbunds or black evening waistcoats are occasionally worn.

  *See also Bow Ties; Eveningwear; White Tie*


## BLOGGING

It can feel like almost everyone has their own blog or vlog, but a personal website can be a lucrative resource when used effectively.

If you're thinking of becoming a blogger, think about what interests you – whether fashion, food or philately. There'll be millions of other people who share your passion, and you'll find it easier to post regularly if you're already enthusiastic and knowledgeable about your subject.

Blogs require regular and effective promotion, but try not to spam friends and family with too many emails or social media posts – although it's fine to elicit their help spreading the word when you're getting started.

When commenting on someone else's blog, keep any observations polite and supportive – remember that somebody will be reading them, so anonymity doesn't give you licence to post thoughtless or offensive remarks.

## BOASTING

The tendency to advertise your own skills, attributes or virtues is immature and bad manners.

While false modesty can also be irritating — a way of eliciting compliments from the unwilling listener — boasting is not an acceptable alternative. If you deserve praise, it will be forthcoming. Nobody receives as many compliments as they would like, and making up for the deficiency by complimenting yourself will only make you unpopular.

*See also Humblebragging*


## BODY LANGUAGE

Your body language is made up of the silent signals that help to determine the impression you give to the world.

Negative signals include crossed arms, hunched shoulders, fiddling and fidgeting.

Positive signals include upright but natural posture, appropriate eye contact (don't stare) and confident hand gestures (no pointing).

During conversation, gently leaning towards the other person and nodding occasionally in agreement conveys interest. A (genuine) smile is always a winner.

Good body language creates a positive air of confidence. It puts others at ease and, according to some research, makes you more sexually attractive.

## BOREDOM

*'Perhaps the world's second worst crime is boredom. The first is being a bore.'*
CECIL BEATON

The weariness that you experience when you are forced to listen to a boring conversation can be quite excruciating. But you must at all costs disguise, or dispense with, the physical manifestations of boredom — yawning, a fixed and glazed look, frequent glances at your phone, or searching for an escape route.

Some people have been known to pour wine over themselves in a desperate attempt to escape the panicky claustrophobia that is brought on by the bore at a party. Others have been forced to lie about mobile phone messages, prior engagements, stomach upsets and domestic emergencies.

Instead, interject, crack a joke, change the course of the conversation or introduce another person into the group. As tempting as it is to fob a bore off onto an unwitting third party, this should only be done in extreme circumstances.

If you have suffered from boredom yourself, you should be aware of the manifestations of boredom in others. You can avoid being a bore by listening to what people have to say and reacting to their conversation. Ask questions and only hold forth if you are invited to do so: keep your obsessions to yourself and never lecture.

Above all, be aware that a proper conversation requires the full participation of at least two people.

### BORROWING

Borrowing is fraught with hazard. Sometimes it is unavoidable, but once you have borrowed from a friend, you have unbalanced your relationship, tipping it from equal peers to that of bank manager and account holder.

If you must borrow money from someone you know, you can manage the situation by setting up a standing order the very day of the loan. Even if it's for a tiny amount each month, the message is clear: that you fully intend to pay back your borrowing.

If you are a borrower of more frivolous items, the lines are a little more blurred. Borrowing a skirt, a book or a pair of earrings can be flattering; it implies that the person from whom you are liberating the item has covetable taste. Just try not to stretch it, shrink it, lose it or spatter it with food, and offer to have it professionally cleaned before returning it.

*See also Lending*

### BOSSES

Our bosses have a major impact on our working lives: the primary reason cited by staff for wanting to leave a particular job is a dislike of their boss.

Good bosses listen to their staff. They recognise strengths, understand procedures (no matter how big or small) and set reasonable goalposts (that they don't shift).

Praise, encouragement and rewards are delivered promptly when due – resulting in high professional morale.

Remember your boss is human – treat him or her with respect but not subservience. If you make a mistake at work, own up to your boss as soon as possible. He or she will appreciate your honesty and may be able to help you contain the consequences of your blunder.

## BOUNCERS

Bouncers should be treated with respect and not argued with; after all, it is in their power to throw you out of the club or refuse you entry if they take a dislike to you. Check the dress code of the club first to avoid disappointment on the night. If a bouncer refuses you entry for any reason, accept this and leave the queue without causing a scene. Only the brave attempt bribery.

## BOW TIES

*'The finest clothing made is a person's skin, but, of course, society demands something more than this.'*
MARK TWAIN

When an invitation states 'black tie', a man is required to wear a dinner jacket and a bow tie. Bow ties should be black and hand-tied — avoid clip-on, novelty or coloured ties.

In other contexts, a bow tie can be a natty and eccentric addition to a smart-casual outfit. Some male professionals such as surgeons also choose to wear them at work if they are unable to wear a necktie for health-and-safety reasons.

How to tie a bow tie:

· Hang the tie around your neck, in place over the collar. Adjust the tie so that one end is slightly longer than the other, crossing the long end over the short.

· Bring the long end through the centre at the neck. Form an angled loop with the short end of the tie crossing left. Drop the long end at the neck over this horizontal loop.

· Form a similar angled loop with the loose long end of the tie and push this loop through the short loop.

· Tighten the knot by adjusting the ends of both loops.

*See also Black Tie*


## BOWING

Bowing is the customary greeting in East Asia, particularly Japan, China, Vietnam and Korea. When you're travelling in these countries, try to demonstrate respect by following suit. In traditional or formal settings, the person who bows lowest is showing the most subservience, which can be useful to know if you're trying to secure business. Check with your host if you're unsure what is most appropriate.

In the UK, men should also bow if they are introduced to a member of the Royal Family. The bow should be made by bending from the neck or shoulders while briefly lowering your eyes. Bow again when the member of the Royal Family leaves.

*See also Queen, HM The; Royal Family*


## BREXIT

Few political developments have divided the nation as much as the UK's decision to leave the EU in the referendum of June 2016, with 'leavers' and 'remainers' seemingly split by generational, geographical and social disparities.

However – and if ever – 'Brexit' finally manifests itself, as a conversation topic it's particularly fraught with hazards. Be wary of raising the subject in conversation with someone you don't know well, or at family gatherings where you wish to maintain a harmonious atmosphere. Don't make any assumptions about how somebody chose to vote – and don't try to find out, unless they volunteer the information.

If it transpires that your views on the subject differ, try to listen to, and understand, the other person's point of view. When expressing your side of the argument, do your best not to get personal or emotional – any rationale will only be undermined if you let your temper and feelings get the better of you.

### BUFFETS

At formal 'wedding-style' buffets, guests get called up table-by-table; get your food promptly when invited, as guests who are slow off the mark can hold up the conveyor belt. At parties with a buffet, timing is less crucial, but make sure you don't end up being the last one chewing. Food may be eaten standing up, so choose a fork-friendly selection that requires little or no cutting.

Plates shouldn't be overloaded – it's better to go back for seconds than look like you haven't eaten for a week. *See also Parties*

### BURPING

In certain cultures, burping is an expression of appreciation for a meal, but in the UK, burping in public is considered rude.

### BUSINESS CARDS

Exchanging business cards is common practice for business introductions and even some social ones.

The standard business card is about the same size as a credit card. Your full name and usually your job title should be printed on it. Qualifications after your name may be added (leave off university degrees), but titles before the name are not usually included.

Contact details such as phone numbers, email and postal address should also appear.

When travelling abroad for work, consider having your business card translated and printed in the relevant language as well as in English, and understand the etiquette of the country you're visiting. In East Asia, for example, business cards are given and received with great deference and care. Present and receive cards with two hands. Look carefully at your contact's card when you receive it, then place it on the table in front of you – don't tuck it away in a back pocket or write comments on it in view of its owner. The business card is seen as representative of your host and his or her role, so treating one casually is seen as hugely disrespectful.

## BUSINESS TRIPS

Going on a business trip with colleagues can often seem to re-draw the automatic lines of office etiquette; you're suddenly in a situation where you're snoozing next to your colleagues on the aeroplane, breakfasting with them, sometimes even sunbathing with them around the pool of the hotel. But don't be fooled by the enforced

intimacy of the trip: work hierarchies still exist. You may have seen your boss in a swimsuit brandishing an elaborate cocktail, but this shouldn't alter your behaviour or respect towards him or her.

If possible, travel to and from the trip separately from your colleagues. Other people always want to do things differently from you – arrive at the airport hours earlier than you would, or chat throughout the flight, for example – and travelling separately will avoid awkwardness. Once there, play the exercise card (especially swimming where it's hard to be sociable while ploughing up and down the pool) to avoid round-the-clock proximity to your workmates.

Above all, adopt a demeanour of benign tolerance for whatever bizarre situation you find yourself in, be it a sauna in Frankfurt or a karaoke bar in Tokyo.

If you are on a solo business trip, don't be afraid to dine alone in the hotel restaurant, but try not to feel self-conscious about your solitude. A book, newspaper or your smartphone can provide distraction, but don't miss out on the (discreet) people-watching opportunities.
*See also Office Politics*

CAMPING TO
CUTLERY

## CAMPING

Be considerate of other campers, and don't encroach on neighbours' pitches. Keep your own space tidy and take home any litter or deposit it in bins on site, recycling where possible.

Use the bathroom facilities provided and clean up after your pets. Avoid loud conversation or music late at night or early in the morning – and remember that canvas provides very little in the way of sound-proofing, so no gossiping about your neighbours.

All outdoor lights should be turned off late at night when your neighbours may want to sleep. Do not start a campfire or barbecue too close to others' pitches.

Where your tent is one of thousands, such as at a music festival, note where you pitched it as well as anything that distinguishes it from others. Carry a torch to avoid stumbling around the campsite after dark, muttering 'I'm sure it was here somewhere'.

## CANAPÉS

Navigate the canapé minefield by adopting a tactical approach. If you're hungry, remember that it is very poor form to take two canapés at a time. Always try and eat a canapé in one mouthful, without overfilling your mouth or chewing vigorously mid-conversation. Watch your timing. Only tuck in when you aren't about to be introduced to someone. If a delicacy looks challenging

or messy, politely decline and wait for something more manageable to appear.

Canapés are often served with complicated sticks, spoons or sauces. Check for discreetly placed dishes where apparatus can be discarded; never put something you've eaten off back on a tray that is still circulating. Equally, never double dip your canapé in the sauce.
*See also Parties*

## CAREER

*'Don't confuse having a career with having a life.'*
HILLARY CLINTON

Manners maketh the future millionaire. Both employers and employees are increasingly acknowledging the importance of what are termed 'soft skills'. Here the emphasis is on an easy grasp of manners, the confidence that comes from knowing the appropriate response in any given situation and an awareness of how your behaviour affects others.

Such skills are initially vital at the interview stage and then crucial in both client situations and for harmonious office relations.

Ideally, those who have honed these skills to the benefit of their careers should remember such manners outside the workplace, too, and realise that their job might not be the most riveting thing for their friends and family. Successful careerists who've started to believe their own propaganda can easily turn into the most boring people in the room, especially to those who might not be in the conventional career mainstream: full-time parents, downsizers, or those who've just lost their own jobs.

## CHAMPAGNE

Open the bottle gently without shaking to avoid spraying the champagne everywhere like a triumphant Formula One driver. Peel off the foil and remove the 'cage' that keeps the cork in place. Ease the cork off by keeping a light hold on it while twisting the bottle slowly – you're aiming for a gentle sigh, not a loud pop. Pour into champagne flutes, which can be filled about three-quarters full. The tall, narrow shape of the glass will preserve the bubbles. Hold it at the stem so your warm hands don't affect the temperature of the champagne.

Champagne should be served chilled, so sit an opened bottle in an ice bucket between refills.

*See also: Prosecco*

## CHAT-UP LINES

'If I said you had a beautiful body, would you hold it against me?'

Male or female, young or not-so-young, chat-up lines are best avoided. Do you really want to be remembered for second-hand conversation? Remember

the basics: eye contact, confidence and humour. Ask them about themselves and remember what they tell you. Make them laugh. Be interested and interesting. Never move things along too quickly or jump the gun.

## CHEWING GUM

Gum has been around in one form or another for 5,000 years (when Neolithic man chewed lumps of birch bark tar), and remains popular now to freshen breath, ease tension, suppress the appetite, or as an aid for quitting smoking.

The problem with chewing gum is not so much in the act of chewing as it is in the act of disposal. Wrap it in paper and throw it away in a bin – don't drop it on the street or stick it to an item of furniture.

Chew gently, with your mouth closed; vigorous mastication looks bovine. Blowing bubbles is for small children only.

## CHILDREN

*'If you bungle raising your children, I don't think whatever else you do matters.'*
JACQUELINE ONASSIS

It's easy to despair that children's behaviour is getting worse, that table manners are a thing of the past, and that respect for elders has gone out of the window.

As a loving parent, we might feel that we should indulge our children's natural impulses at all costs, but don't forget that children respond to structure and boundaries and need to be taught how to behave from a young age.

We teach our children to walk, we teach them to talk and, if we want our children to interact successfully, we teach them manners: not just elbows-in, saying-thank-you manners, but how to get along with others.

There is no consensus, however, over how to raise a well-mannered child. Some children are revered as demi-gods whose will must never be contravened, while others belong to the manners drummed-in, seen-but-not-heard camp.

Steering a middle course is clearly tricky, but there are some universal boundaries to be set. The parent's mantra should be, 'Is my child behaving in a way that's annoying anyone?' Never fall into the trap of imagining that your idea of what's annoying is the same as everyone else's. A child singing their favourite song over and over again can be a cute party trick at home, but is likely just to irritate others.

Above all, teach by example: it's no good telling your child off for interrupting, shouting or using bad language if you do exactly the same in their presence.

## CHOPSTICKS

If your chopstick technique is unreliable and you find yourself asking for a fork instead, it's a good idea to

practise at home. Wooden chopsticks are usually better at gripping than the plastic versions.

Hold the chopsticks parallel in one hand. Your thumb and forefinger hold and manipulate the top stick. Your middle finger rests between the sticks, keeping the bottom stick held still. The top stick is manoeuvred by the thumb and forefinger to grip food and bring it to your mouth. The truly skilled can master picking up shelled peanuts.

Place your chopsticks by the right-hand side of your plate when you are not using them; you may be provided with special rests. Don't use chopsticks to pass food to people or to point at others. Avoid leaving them sticking up in a bowl of rice or noodles – in East Asia, this is seen as mimicking an offering to the dead.

*See also Sushi*


## CHRISTENINGS

A church christening (known officially as baptism) welcomes a child (or adult) into the faith of that church. Parents, relatives, the chosen godparents and close friends attend, and the day should be treated as a formal occasion. Non-religious ceremonies are known as naming parties or naming ceremonies.

Christenings often take place during a normal Sunday service. If you aren't a regular church-goer, attempt to engage with the service, and avoid looking bored. Dress smartly – jeans are usually not appropriate, but if in doubt, check with the child's parents.

A gift for the child may be presented to the parents. A small, white leather-bound bible is traditional, as is silverware – such as a charm bracelet or engraved picture frame. If you wish to go down a less traditional route, simply ensure that the gift is a keepsake that can be treasured by the child in the years to come.

*See also Godparents; Presents*


## CHRISTMAS CARDS

Choose your cards carefully. Remember that humorous cards, or cards with religious messages inside, may not be appreciated by everybody. It may be a good idea to buy two sets – one for those who will enjoy a light-hearted, fun card, and another with a generic 'Season's Greetings' inside.

Email cards could be inappropriate for an elderly relative, but may be acceptable for younger friends or colleagues.

Include both forenames and surname if necessary, to clarify who the card is from, eg. 'Best wishes, John and Jenny Smith'. Nowadays, the order of names is a matter of personal choice.

It is fine to include a brief line – such as 'we must catch up in the new year' – but avoid writing an essay or circulating a 'round robin' newsletter. Instead, you could include a short, personal letter on a separate sheet to friends or relatives who are rarely seen.

If you miss the post, or receive a last-minute card from someone not on your list, then send a brief note, card or postcard with your best wishes. Alternatively, send a new year's card. It is a matter of personal choice whether you send cards at all, but remember that people who send them to you may be surprised not to receive one back.
*See also Greeting Cards*

## CLUBS, PRIVATE MEMBERS'

*'I refuse to join any club that would have me as a member.'*
GROUCHO MARX

If you're a member of a club, try not to boast about it. If you're inviting guests, be aware that they may not know what to expect and keep them informed: is there a dress code, or any other rules? Accompany them into the club or meet them at the door so you can sign them in. If you are a visitor yourself, respect the club's codes of conduct.

Dress appropriately and, as a general rule, don't tip the staff.

## COLD CALLERS

The bane of many people's existence, cold callers are an invasive nuisance, especially when their calls come during antisocial, out-of-office hours. Dealing with

them, however, should never be an excuse for rudeness.

If you don't recognise the number of the person calling you, you're well within your rights to ignore the call and let it go to voicemail. If you do pick up, remember that the person on the other end is simply doing a job, and answer them politely and firmly. Intercept their sales pitch with a courteous 'I'm sorry, I'm really not interested/this is not a convenient time...' and hang up.

## COLLEAGUES

Support your workmates and they will do the same for you. If you can see someone is particularly busy or stressed, there may be some way you can help without affecting your own workload too much. Always be willing to dedicate time and effort to your relationships with colleagues. This may mean giving up an evening for after-work drinks or going out for lunch together once in a while.

Not all topics of conversation are suitable for the office, especially in an open plan environment, so don't embarrass your colleagues by discussing inappropriate or personal topics, and resist the temptation to gossip about other members of staff.

Try to keep a balance between your work life and your private life; discretion dictates that you retain some areas of privacy (and intimate personal calls at your desk

are never a good idea), but it is also vital that you open up a little and find some common ground.

*See also: Desk, Dining at One's, Office Parties, Office Politics, Office Romance*

## COMPETITIVENESS

To be competitive is both drummed into us from birth and almost as immediately decried as being an unattractive character trait. The achievements of our contemporaries – from potty training to A-levels – are held up as an example, but if our desire to win is too obvious or overzealous we are reprimanded.

The same paradox exists in the world of work: out-performing the competition is one thing, being seen to do it in a pushy way is quite another.

As Ovid commented 2,000 years ago, 'Like man, a horse never runs so fast as when he has other horses to catch up and outpace.' Competition can raise your game – the trick is not to alienate others while you're climbing.

No matter what the field – be it the workplace or the PTA – identify both a mentor and a mentee, and create a team around you: this will position you as a natural leader of others. To achieve this, your armoury will require plentiful supplies of two weapons: charm and knowledge. If you know what's what, who's who and here's how, then you're on the way.

## COMPLAINING

*'When people cease to complain, they cease to think.'*
NAPOLEON

The British love to complain, but we're not very good at it. Although we like a good whinge, we're more likely to moan at someone else than complain directly, in a way that might actually fix the problem.

The best approach for complaining effectively is one of polite persistence. If the person to whom you're speaking isn't offering any form of resolution or compensation, ask to speak to his or her manager. Try, if at all possible, to resolve the complaint there and then rather than being fobbed off by the advice to write a letter or send an email.

When complaining in person, be as discreet as possible, and don't resort to aggression – if you feel yourself losing your temper, remove yourself from the situation and revisit it later, when you feel calmer.

If you are forced to lodge a complaint by email or via an online form, don't let the guise of anonymity tempt you to give rein to your inner troll. Remember that an actual person will read your message, so be just as polite as you would be over the phone. Bear in mind that emails can be recirculated indefinitely, so don't write anything you might regret.

On the phone, resist the temptation to vent your frustrations at the person who answers your call. The fault likely lies further up the food chain, so keep your comments objective and neutral rather than personal.

Being rude will most likely cause the other person to become defensive and reluctant to help, whereas politeness and a willingness to work with them to find a solution are often disarming. Sometimes all you have to do is smile confidently and say, 'I'm sure we can resolve this,' or subtly remind them of the reputation they have to uphold.

## COMPLIMENTS

A genuine compliment will make the recipient feel great about themselves, and oils the wheels of social intercourse.

Only offer compliments when you believe them, and don't over-compliment — you will look like an insincere flatterer.

Stick to specifics; vague, overgeneralised compliments such as 'you're such a great person' are easily devalued. Never damn with faint praise ('I'm really surprised by what you've managed to throw together!'), or give a compliment with one hand and take away with the other.

A timely and spontaneous compliment feels more genuine than one issued as an afterthought — don't wait until you are leaving a dinner party to praise the food, for example.

If you are the recipient of a compliment, smile and say thank you. Don't denigrate yourself, or take it as a cue for boasting. Never retaliate with a knee-jerk compliment back. The recipient will, rightly, regard it with suspicion.

*See also Flattery*

## CONVERSATION

Being a good conversationalist is a valuable social skill, enabling you to put people at ease and ensuring you will be remembered for your tact and good humour. Mastering the art of conversation will ensure you are never short of invitations to dinner or parties.

A good conversationalist strikes a balance between talking and listening. They pick up threads to create a multilayered conversation and a sense of intimacy – the other person feels sure that they are interested.

It is important to set the conversation off well. Try to think of an alternative to the usual 'How are you?' or 'What do you do?', but there is no need to launch immediately into contentious issues such as religion or politics. Gentle humour and the occasional well-placed compliment all make conversation easier.

Ask questions, but don't conduct an interview – there is a fine line between interest and intrusion. Familiarity comes with time, so be aware of unspoken barriers.

Avoid strong opinion or stark honesty; an occasional frisson is interesting, but controversial views may offend.

## COUGHING

Follow coughing etiquette: turn away from other people; if possible cough into a handkerchief or tissue, not your hand; if you do not have a handkerchief, cover your mouth with your hand.

If possible, stay away from public performances — especially concerts or plays — to avoid irritating fellow members of the audience. Ensure you're equipped with an emergency supply of cough sweets.

If coughing is unavoidable, use other sounds to mask it (applause, loud music, laughter).

## CRYING

*'Heaven knows we need never be ashamed of our tears, for they are rain upon the blinding dust of earth, overlying our hard hearts.'*
CHARLES DICKENS

In the past, the expression of emotion — especially by men — was frowned upon, but crying is now accepted as a healthy and therapeutic response to bereavement, pain or sadness.

Seeing someone in tears can cause others to feel alarmed or panicked. Remember that crying is not always a sign of intense distress — it may be an involuntary expression of anger, frustration or disappointment — and drawing attention to it may make the situation worse.

Gently check if the other person is OK, and see if they would like to talk in a quiet place. Don't persist or swamp them with sympathy if they say they are fine, but do follow up later on.

If you notice that someone is frequently tearful and upset, there may be something more serious going on.

If speaking to the person doesn't help, you might need to involve others — a member of your HR team if you're at work, or a partner, close friend or family member.

## CUTLERY

A knife should be held firmly in your right hand, with the handle tucked into your palm, your thumb down one side of the handle and your index finger along the top (but never touching the top of the blade). It should never be eaten off or held like a pencil.

When used with a knife or spoon, the fork should be held in the left hand, in much the same way as the knife, with the prongs facing downwards. On its own, it is held in the right hand, with the prongs facing upwards, resting on the fingers and secured with the thumb and index finger.

A spoon is held in the right hand, resting on the fingers and secured with the thumb and index finger. Food should be eaten off the side of the spoon; it should never be used at a right angle to the mouth.

Cutlery should be rested on the plate/bowl between bites, and placed together in the bottom-centre when you are finished.

If you're baffled by the amount of cutlery at your place setting, you can usually start with the utensils on the outside and move in. The pudding spoon and fork will usually be laid above your plate.

*See also Table Manners; Table Settings*

DANCING TO
DRY, GOING

## DANCING

As the evening progresses you may think you're becoming a better dancer, but the opposite is usually true. If you've turned into a sweaty, uncoordinated muddle of limbs it is time to call it a night.

Equally, if you find yourself alone on the dance floor it may be wise to exit, unless your Travolta-esque routine has drawn an admiring crowd.

There are certain occasions when you should make an effort to participate. If you are at a wedding or party and everyone else is dancing it would look antisocial to sit at the side. You will get lost in the crowd, so don't worry about looking foolish. If you are not a confident dancer, start by moving your feet from side to side in time with the music — just be careful not to tread on anyone else's toes.

If you are out with one other person, don't leave them sitting on the sidelines while you take to the dance floor. They may quickly become bored, or, worse still, find another dance partner.

## DATING

If you've asked someone out, it's up to you to make the arrangements. Give some thought to what the other person might enjoy, and keep it simple on a first date: drinks or coffee are safer options than a meal. You can always go on somewhere if the date's going well.

If you are running late, give as much notice as possible, preferably by phone. Being up to 15 minutes late should not be a problem, and a brief apology will be fine. Being more than half an hour late looks like rudeness unless you have a genuine excuse.

Cancelling a date should be done as far in advance as possible. At the same time, make sure you rearrange for another time in the near future.

If you are stood up, try not to take it personally: maintain your dignity and don't resort to angry texts. Reassure yourself that you have made a lucky escape and move on.

On a date, switch your phone to silent and keep it out of temptation's way. Ask plenty of questions and try to be open, chatty and positive. Don't talk about exes or dwell on past dating experiences.

Paying the bill is the responsibility of the inviter, at least on the first occasion. As things progress it is fine to take turns settling the bill.

*See also Online Dating*

## DEATH

The logistical challenges that surround a death — from the bureaucratic nightmare of registering it, to the frenzy of the funeral arrangements — can often disguise the impact of the death itself.

Death affects different people in different ways, and in the absence of a strict social rulebook dictating how to behave after someone has died, many of us are at a loss as to how to address the subject or how to treat our bereaved friends or loved ones.

The immediate aftermath of the death is often more straightforward to navigate; the bereaved is either concealing grief with activity or is so shocked and upset that your presence alone is enough.

Children should not be excluded from the process or they may feel confused and worried that the death is somehow their fault.

Later on, avoid the temptation to wrap death in euphemism: using terms like 'departed' or 'moved over' when writing a letter of condolence, for example. Instead aim for a frank and confiding tone, dwelling nostalgically and fondly on past happier days.

The tough part of death — and grieving — is that it doesn't stop at the funeral. The best thing you can do as a friend is to realise this. Support in the early days of death is a given — but maintaining those levels of support one, two, or three years on is where true friendship counts.

## DESK, EATING AT ONE'S

As we all live busier, hyper-connected lives, the concept of dining 'al-Desko' is increasingly replacing the time-honoured lunch break.

Absent-mindedly munching on a sandwich while staring at your screen may leave you feeling unsatisfied.

You'll also find that you're more productive if you can take a break — however brief — rather than working through lunch, only to hit a slump at 3pm.

If you must eat lunch at your desk, consider your co-workers: choose food that's not too smelly or messy, and be wary of making loud chewing and crunching sounds or involuntary moans of appreciation. Clean up afterwards to avoid a sticky keyboard.

## DIETS

The popularity and variety of diets continue to grow — from celebrity-fronted cookery books and exercise plans to the more pervasive trend of 'clean eating', which advocates exotic replacements for any number of supposed nutritional offenders, including dairy, gluten, carbohydrates and sugar.

While both men and women are increasingly conditioned to seek the perfect body, dieting, in the sense of restricting one or more food groups, rarely works in the long-term. A permanent change of lifestyle and mindset is more effective in ensuring that any weight loss is not short-lived.

If you are on a diet, don't assume that others will be interested in your recipe for kale salad or cauliflower rice. Avoid the temptation to be evangelical and don't expect your host to cater specially for you.

The appropriate response on hearing that a friend or

loved one is on a diet is to offer constant support and praise — 'Wow, yes, you look thinner already'.

In fact, your heart is probably sinking: your once entertaining friend or loved one is about to trans-mogrify into a bore, a human calculator of calorie-counting, a dinner party guest from hell who is going to pick at the food you have slaved over. Take a deep breath and brace yourself for the post-diet recriminations and guilt complexes.

*See also Weight, Discussing*

## DINNER PARTIES

*'At a dinner party one should eat wisely but not too well, and talk well but not too wisely.'*
W. SOMERSET MAUGHAM

When hosting a dinner party, do as much as you can before the guests arrive. Lay the table, sort out the crockery and prepare as much food as possible — you will be able to spend more time with your guests rather than in the kitchen.

Offer guests a drink upon arrival. Spirits should be available as well as wine and beer. A glass of champagne or prosecco is also a good option.

If someone brings a bottle, you may like to open it at some point in the evening, but have your own supply ready in case your guests don't bring wine. If you do not open your guests' wine on the night, you might want to tell them discreetly that it is too exceptional for the assembled group and that you're saving it for a special occasion.

A table plan is a good way of organising your guests, but can look over-formal. If you want the atmosphere to feel laid back, let people choose where they want to sit; just make sure that couples are separated. Keep an eye on the conversational dynamic during the first two courses; if your guests aren't meshing, suggest everyone moves round for the pudding.

If you are invited to a dinner party, RSVP promptly (mentioning any dietary requirements you may have), and give as much notice as possible if you need to cancel.

Never arrive early to a dinner party. A few minutes after the time stated on the invitation is polite; if you are going to be more than 15 minutes late, phone ahead and warn your host.

It is polite to take a gift; chocolates, flowers, or a bottle of wine are all good choices. Take a couple of bottles if there are two of you. Write or call to say thank you as soon as possible after the event.

*See also Hosts and Hostesses*

## DIVORCE

It may be hard to imagine introducing manners into the divorce courts, but civilised separation – or 'conscious uncoupling' as Gwyneth Paltrow and Chris Martin would have it – is possible if both parties are prepared to co-operate and compromise.

Your number one priority should be any children you have together, so try to keep a lid on any acrimony when you're with them. Once you have sought advice from lawyers and decided on a course of action, sit down with your children together to explain calmly what is happening and what it will mean for them. Keep any negotiations between the two of you and never be tempted to bad-mouth your spouse to your children.

When it comes to the terms of your divorce, try to resolve more minor disagreements between the two of you to avoid wasting lawyers' time (and your money). You may find mediation helpful in this regard.

Try not to force friends or family members to choose sides, and be discreet and sensitive to the feelings of your ex if you're introducing a new partner into social circles.

As a good friend or close relative of a couple in the throes of a divorce, you will need to be patient, tolerant and diplomatic. You will also have to master the art of being non-committal, which enables you to say supportive things without entirely writing off the ex-partner – insurance against a passionate reunion at a later date.

*See also Ending a Relationship*

## DOGGIE BAGS

Requesting a doggie bag used to be seen as an American habit, but as we become increasingly mindful of food waste, it has become more acceptable to do so in the UK too.

The decision will partly depend on the type of establishment you are visiting — asking if you can take away uneaten food is less likely to raise eyebrows in a pizzeria than it is in a Michelin-starred restaurant.

When the waiter comes to clear your plates, explain that you enjoyed the food but couldn't finish it, and ask if he or she can box up any leftovers for you to take home. Be wary of trying to transport anything too smelly — or likely to leak into your lap — on the way home.

## DOGS

*'The most affectionate creature in the world is a wet dog.'*
AMBROSE BIERCE

You may love your dog, applaud its barking and tolerate its bowel movements, but you are making a mistake if you assume the rest of the world feels the same.

When you are out with your dog, keep it under control. Be aware that small children, and some adults, are very frightened of dogs, so if yours runs up to strangers enthusiastically, call it away or drag it off with a polite apology.

If you have any respect at all for your fellow human beings, carry a supply of plastic bags to clean up any mess when walking your dog. You may feel foolish and humiliated as you clean up after it, but choosing to be a pet owner means accepting full responsibility for everything it does.

## DOORS, HOLDING OPEN

Men holding doors open for women is still a polite gesture, but if a woman arrives at the door first and starts to open it, a man shouldn't awkwardly rush in front of her exclaiming 'I'll get that!'

Both genders should hold doors open (and check) for people coming through behind them.

## DRIVING

A car is a potentially lethal weapon, and a good driver will always remember this before using it as a way of expressing irritation, frustration or red-blooded rage. Aggressive driving should be avoided at all costs: tailgating, with or without flashing headlights, and pointless horn-blowing are not signs of superiority, merely an inability to control emotions while in charge of a very powerful machine.

Good driving manners mean being aware of other

motorists. Let other cars into the queue in front of you with a friendly wave or flash of the headlights – a graceful gesture that will only cost you seconds. Give way to oncoming traffic. Indicate when overtaking. Acknowledge other motorists' gestures – it will make crowded, frustrating roads seem infinitely more civilised.

Breaking the speed limit is dangerous, but hesitant kerb-crawling can be very annoying for drivers caught behind you. Don't allow yourself to be distracted by your SatNav or your sound system, and if you must answer phone calls, make sure you use hands-free.

Be aware of other road-users. Always give cyclists plenty of leeway and slow down when approaching pedestrian crossings – if you make plenty of allowances for unpredictable behaviour you should be able to curb your antagonism and help to make the roads a safer place.

If you are a passenger, never turn into a back-seat driver: you may be ashen-faced with fear, but stamping on imaginary brakes and shouting commands are not going to help. Lead by example, and keep calm and collected.
*See also Road Rage; Zebra Crossings*

## DRUNKENNESS

At the beginning of the evening, drink is the ally of social confidence; by the end, it is the enemy of social manners. One minute, drinking makes you feel on top of the world. The next, you're punctuating your sentences with hiccups and staring blearily into your phone screen as you try to compose a message to your ex.

There's a difference between an enjoyable state of intoxicated merriment and the kind of drunkenness that brings introspection, neediness and over-emotionalism. We all know that moderation is the mother of good sense, that we should be happy enough with our one or two glasses of wine.

The good news is that drinking-without-drunkenness is possible: eat well, alternate alcoholic drinks with glasses of water, never get drunker than your love interest and know your limits – the graceful drunk is always thinking beyond their immediate environment, alert to the warning signs of impending intoxication, and ready to go home before an enjoyable evening ends in tears or belligerence.

If you are handling a drunk who has failed to take this path, proceed with caution. The most important thing is to stop them driving home, so call them a cab and try to persuade them to consume some food and water.

Don't bother berating them while they're still intoxicated – they won't remember it in the morning. It's up to your conscience whether you resist the temptation to torment them with tales of their tipsiness the following day.

*See also Dry, Going; Office Parties*

DRY, GOING

*'Once, during Prohibition, I was forced to live for days on nothing but food and water.'*
W. C. FIELDS

Between Dry January, Stoptober and NOvember, more and more of us are choosing to forego alcohol for extended periods at a time.

If you know someone who has given up alcohol, whether for lifestyle or medical reasons, respect their decision and don't try to lure them into falling off the wagon.

As a host, you may be secretly disappointed that a guest isn't drinking, but you must never let this show — meet their refusal with good grace, and offer a tempting range of alcohol-free drinks.

If you are the teetotaller (however temporary), you must also mind your manners. Refuse a drink politely and give an explanation if you think that helps, but don't feel you have to.

Never act the martyr, miserably cradling your mineral water as the party takes off around you, and don't lecture others about the benefits of an alcohol-free existence.

If you are sober, intoxicated company can be baffling; conversations meander, arguments break out for no reason, non-jokes are met with general hilarity. If the prospect of this horrifies you, it's probably best to take a pass on that party invitation.

If, however, you can endure — and even enjoy — these antics, you will be worth your weight in gold — the one

sober guest at the end of the evening who is able to sort
out the increasingly unruly guests, and even drive them
safely home.

*See also Drunkenness*

EAVESDROPPING TO
EYEBROWS

## EAVESDROPPING

*'There's nothing like eavesdropping to show you that the world outside your head is different from the world inside.'*
THORNTON WILDER

Listening in to other people's private conversations is ill-advised, but highly tempting. If you must eavesdrop, make sure that you never reveal how you've come by your information. If you are fascinated by a conversation at the next table, avoid the obvious signs of eavesdropping: cocked head, frequent glances and the distracted inability to participate in your own conversation. Resist all urges to gatecrash the discussion – 'Excuse me, I couldn't help but hear ...' Your victims will, rightly, be outraged.

If you're an inveterate eavesdropper, it is easier, and more polite, to indulge yourself by listening in to other people's mobile phone conversations. They're going on all around you, they're frequently intimate and revealing, and the people on the phone who are loudly broadcasting their secrets don't even seem to mind you listening.

## ELBOWS

Keep your elbows tucked into your sides when eating, and make sure that they don't encroach on the space of the person beside you. Don't lean on your elbows when eating – although it is fine to rest them on the table when you do not have utensils in your hands.
*See also Table Manners*

## EMAIL

Many of us are now slaves to our bulging inboxes, so before you send an email, ask yourself whether you could call the recipient on the phone or speak to them in person instead. You might find your enquiry gets more attention.

When you're sending an email, remember that your message may be stored permanently, and that there is no such thing as confidentiality in cyberspace. Sensitive communications should therefore be sent by other means. Think carefully before hitting 'send' if the message is written in haste or when emotions are running high. Avoid sarcasm and subtle humour unless you know that the reader will 'get it'. If in doubt, err towards the polite and formal. Use emojis and 'x's with caution in professional correspondence or when you are not well acquainted with the recipient.

Where there is more than one recipient, list them alphabetically or, in the business environment, according to hierarchy. This applies also to the 'cc' line. Avoid blind copying ('bcc') where possible: instead, forward the original email on to the third party, with a short note explaining any confidentiality. Blind copying is, however, appropriate for distribution lists, for example, where all recipients must remain anonymous.

If you send an email in error, phone the recipient and ask them to ignore/delete the message. It is polite to

reply to emails promptly – a simple acknowledgement
with a promise that you will give the email your full
attention at a given later point is preferable to 'sitting
on' the message.

*See also Emojis; Handwritten; Punctuation*

## EMOJIS

Emojis tend to divide opinion – their detractors
see them as irritating, childish and unnecessary,
while those in favour consider them a harmless and
playful shorthand.

If you fall on the former side of the argument, be
tolerant of emojis and learn to interpret them – bar a
few obscure exceptions, they tend to be fairly self-
explanatory. You might even be persuaded to throw a
smiley face or two into your responses for good measure
– a stonily formal reply to a barrage of emojis can seem
hostile. If you're an infrequent user, check with a
trusted friend before hitting 'send' on a series of
jaunty-looking hand gestures.

If you're an emoji fan, use them discriminately –
avoid their use in professional correspondence except
with close colleagues, and don't overload your messages
or social media posts with them or they will begin to lose
their efficacy.

*See also Email*

## ENDING A RELATIONSHIP

There is no happy way to end a relationship, but if you can bring yourself to be direct, decisive and kind, you will stand a better chance of getting away with your dignity intact.

Always break up with someone in person; an email or text message looks cowardly and impersonal. Once face-to-face, don't allow ambiguity to enter the conversation or offer any crumbs of mercy that could imply you're prepared to get back together in the future.

It is much better to be regretful but honest. Above all, don't spin out the conversation too long – keep it brief, make sure the other person is OK, and then leave.

If you're on the receiving end of a break-up, the shock can be overwhelming – you may feel tearful, furious or completely at a loss. Whatever your reaction, the prospect of embarking on another relationship seems completely unfeasible.

Speak to a close friend or family member, try to keep busy, and allow yourself some time to get over the relationship. Don't be tempted to follow your ex's movements on social media – if necessary, unfriend them or block their updates. Consider deleting their number from your phone so that you're not tempted to send a wistful message after a few drinks.

*See also Divorce*

## ENGAGEMENT

It is usual for a newly engaged couple to share the news with their parents first; they should then spread the word to other family, friends and colleagues. Ensure that important people hear the news from you personally rather than via social media.

The engagement may then be announced publicly in the 'Forthcoming Marriages' column of a local or national newspaper. This was traditionally organised by the bride's parents, with the wording reading:

*Mr P Jennings and Miss K Ashton–Smythe*
*The engagement is announced between Peter, second son of Mr and Mrs Simon Jennings of Lewes, East Sussex, and Katherine, only daughter of Mr and Mrs John Ashton–Smythe of Godalming, Surrey.*

This wording is altered as appropriate for same-sex couples.

In days gone by, the mother of the groom-to-be wrote to the bride-to-be's parents, expressing her happiness at the engagement. Nowadays, this is not necessary, but it makes sense for the two families to be in touch soon after the engagement.

Once the engagement is made public, friends will often send a letter or card of congratulations, but if you've posted the news on social media, congratulations may well come via the same channel.

Many couples will celebrate with an engagement party,

which might be hosted by one or both sets of parents, or by the couple themselves. If the bride-to-be's father is a host, he may make an informal speech and toast the couple. Presents are not expected, but a small token is a nice gesture.

If an engagement is called off, there is usually no need for a detailed explanation. If a formal announcement is necessary, the wording should read:

*The marriage arranged between Mr Peter Jennings and Miss Kate Ashton-Smythe will not take place.*

If wedding invitations have already been sent out, informal notes or printed cards should be sent to each guest announcing that the ceremony will not take place.

The engagement ring and any presents the former bride-to-be has given her fiancé should be returned. Any wedding presents received should be returned with a letter of thanks.

*See also Marriage; Presents; Proposals*


## ENTRANCES

While you may want your arrival at a social event to be duly noted, don't overdo it. Breezing straight in to interrupt an interesting conversation, boldly buttonholing the guest of honour, or making an obvious beeline for the drinks or food will cause raised eyebrows.

On the other hand, loitering self-consciously and

waiting to be noticed won't persuade people to talk to you. Walk in confidently and make yourself known to the host and hostess. Take time to assess the ambience of the event before braving a conversational approach.
*See also Exits*


## ENVIRONMENT, RESPECTING THE

There are many ways to make small, everyday changes to your lifestyle for the benefit of the environment. You might find that your finances are better off, too.

Opt for low-energy light bulbs and ensure that your home is well insulated to save energy. Switch off lights when not in use, and only boil as much water as you need.

Where possible, try to buy food that is local and seasonal, and avoid products that use excessive packaging. Bring your own carrier bags when you shop.

Reduce your contribution to landfill by using recycling and composting facilities. Donate unwanted goods to second-hand shops.

Try walking, cycling or using public transport occasionally instead of taking the car. When replacing your car, consider choosing an electric vehicle, especially if you live in a busy city or town.

Already an enviro-expert? You know it makes sense, but resist the temptation to preach to the unconverted …
*See also Recycling*

### EVENINGWEAR

The dress code for a formal evening event will usually be specified as white tie, black tie or, less frequently, lounge suits.

White tie is the most glamorous and formal, and is usually reserved for state banquets and ambassadorial functions. Women would usually be expected to wear a ball gown.

Black tie can be used to describe formal evening dress generally, but it requires a black dinner suit with a white dress shirt and black bow tie. For women, a cocktail dress (long or short) is appropriate. It doesn't have to be black.

'Lounge suits' is less formal, but for men, a suit, shirt and tie are still expected. The equivalent for women usually means a dress or a skirt or trouser suit.

*See also Black Tie; White Tie*

### EXCUSES

*'I attribute my success to this: I never gave or took an excuse.'*
FLORENCE NIGHTINGALE

We live in a world padded out with meaningless excuses that merely muffle and annoy. Leaves on the line, the wrong sort of snow, the ubiquitous signal failure — transport excuses alone have turned us all into cynics.

If you are the person attempting to dodge something or someone, making excuses can often seem the polite

way out. You don't want to tell someone you simply
don't *want* to meet them, or help them out, or come to
their charity evening – because to do so would be rude
– so you make an excuse.

Inventing elaborate excuses, such as a terrible stomach
bug, or a prior engagement, is asking for trouble – in the
privacy-free age of social media, there's every chance
your lie will be exposed. Sticking more closely to the
truth – for example, 'I've been rushing around all week
and I'm just not in the mood for socialising,' may sound
overly blunt, but you won't have to remember which
excuse you made the next time you see the inviter.

As for making excuses about your own behaviour, this is
best avoided. Benjamin Disraeli's famous comment,
'Never complain and never explain,' is based on the
strength and confidence conveyed by knowing when to
stop talking. Excusing a poor performance on the grounds
of ill-health, extenuating circumstances or somebody
else's error only makes you look weak.
*See also Flaking*


**EXES**

*'Experience is the name everyone gives to his mistakes.'*
WOODROW WILSON

Good behaviour is paramount when dealing with your
ex. Revenge tactics or bad-mouthing will only make you

look bitter. If you bump into your ex, be polite and cheerful, and if you find the encounter painful, make your excuses and leave.

When meeting a partner's ex, or an ex's new partner, mature good manners are the best policy. Don't make scathing comments; you'll appear insecure.

If you wish to maintain good relations with your ex, you will have to accept and be friendly towards their new partner. Be completely honest with your current partner; they will need reassurance that no feelings remain between you.

Group meetings are best when dealing with exes; constant one-to-ones are never going to look innocent.

## EXITS

Leave decisively: don't loiter in the hallway, coat on, prevaricating. Once you've decided to leave, say your goodbyes to other guests, and then thank your host or hostess before heading for the door. Having a taxi booked or a particular train to catch can help avoid lengthy farewells.

If you are leaving mid-event, make your departure swift and discreet, ensuring that you do not precipitate the end of the party. If you are the last person left, and your hosts are visibly wilting, you have probably outstayed your welcome. Now is the time to make your exit.

*See also Entrances*

## EYE CONTACT

Generally, eye contact is a good thing: an effective way of establishing trust and rapport with another person. Jobseekers are taught to maintain firm eye contact with their interviewers; children are told to look someone in the eye if they speak to them; everyone agrees that catching a barman's eye is the best way to get served.

There are exceptions, however. In a sauna, shower or other gym situation, eye contact with anything other than the wall or your own navel is construed at best as a come-on, at worst as an affront.

If you're so obsessed with maintaining eye contact in an interview or on a date that you actually forget to maintain the conversation, then any good will be undone.

Remember that there's a mere blink between gazing and staring. Staring is never good. To a drunk, the tiniest glance can seem like aggressive staring, so avoid eye contact in such situations.

Catching someone's eye on a train, in a bar or in the park can be interpreted as an invitation to conversation whether you like it or not, so prepare for the consequences.

## EYEBROWS

Keep eyebrows maintained. Thick, dark and defined eyebrows may be in vogue, but bushy monobrows are not a good look on anyone. Nor is the startled expression that comes from over-plucking.

# F

FACIAL EXPRESSIONS
TO FUNERALS

## FACIAL EXPRESSIONS

The stereotype of the British stiff upper lip, which traditionally precluded us from expressing visible emotion, has been relaxed, and allowing a natural warmth, sympathy or humour to show in your reactions can put others at ease.

Never forget, however, the simple power of the calculated facial gesture: lifting an eyebrow to express contempt or skepticism, pursing one's lips to suggest disapproval – deployed with care, these minute movements can discreetly put others in their place.

## FAILURE

*'I haven't failed. I've just found ten thousand ways that don't work.'*
THOMAS EDISON

While failure can be something quantifiable – missing a target at work, getting fired, not passing an exam – more often it is less tangible, a nagging sense of not living up to our own benchmarks of success.

Feeling like a failure is compounded by the images of success we're shown on a daily basis on our social media feeds – the artful brunch, the gym selfie, the pregnancy and engagement announcements. Remember that few people choose to broadcast the many disappointing, underwhelming or simply dull parts of their daily lives.

On the other hand, genuine, soul-crushing failure is an unfortunate fact of life, and you will react to it far more

kindly in others and in yourself if you recognise this fact.

*Schadenfreude*, the malicious enjoyment of others' failure, is tempting, but should never be apparent to others. Passing judgement on someone because they have failed at something doesn't advance the sum of human happiness.

The way in which we react to failure – and the lessons we learn from it – are far more valuable life experiences than sailing through on a complacent wave of success and ease.

## FAKE TAN

Leave your fake tan to the professionals; orange knees, streaks and bronzed palms are just some of the hazards of amateur fake tanning. Ask your friends if they think you're overdoing it.

Some people don't know when to stop, but it would be the height of bad manners to point this out.

## FASHION

*'Every generation laughs at the old fashions, but follows religiously the new.'*
HENRY DAVID THOREAU

The speed with which fashions move on and evolve can be daunting, but thankfully fashion is no longer prescriptive: it is not about what 'goes together' – if it feels good to you, you're probably doing something right.

Don't fall for the falsehood that, just because something has a designer label attached, it will automatically suit you. There's a fine line between looking stylish and looking like a fashion victim.

The key to fashion is allowing one's eye to adjust to what's new and applying it carefully to one's own look, rather than buying the latest creations that appear on the catwalks or, worse, lingering in a fashion rut.

## FAUX PAS

*'If I could drop dead right now, I'd be the happiest man alive.'*
SAMUEL GOLDWYN

Whether it's asking someone when they're due when they're not actually pregnant, or commiserating with a colleague on his redundancy when he doesn't even know he's about to be fired, faux pas are lurking at every turn.

Embarrassing social blunders are inevitable, but it's how you react to one, or recover from committing one, that dictates whether it will then become a harmless anecdote or a fiery brand of shame.

If you're on the receiving end of a foot-in-mouth moment, the temptation is to be British and polite — a tinkling laugh and a brushing-off the 'When is it due?' question, for example. But the offender is well aware that you are just putting a brave face on their rudeness, which makes them feel worse.

Better all-round is to make a joke about their faux pas, answering, 'No, I'm just hugely fat.' It gently mocks them for asking such an absurd and dangerous question, while also implying that you really don't care what they think, thereby letting them off the hook for the faux pas in the first place.

If you are the one who has made the gaffe, apologising profusely or attempting to explain it is likely to compound the insult. Self-deprecation will lighten the mood and always makes other people feel better. Admit that you're a tactless oaf, make a joke of it. Take comfort from the fact that you are not alone and that, handled deftly, this can become an amusing story for both you and your victim.

### FIRST IMPRESSIONS

It's a truism that it takes seven seconds to make a first impression, but it can also take a lifetime to erase a bad first impression.

To make a good, and lasting, impression the first time you meet someone, always focus on other people; don't try to make yourself the centre of attention. Listen carefully and make direct eye contact. Speak clearly, and respond immediately to what is being said.

Ask questions, and listen to the answers. Try hard to remember the name of the person you have been introduced to, and use it at least once (overuse can look smarmy).

## FIRST NAMES, USE OF

The use – or not – of first names tends to be generational; the older you are, the more you think it natural to be Mr, Mrs, Ms or Miss.

At some point in the middle, you come to expect your title and surname in your dealings with professional people: when seeing a doctor, a lawyer or the head-teacher at your child's school.

The use of first names is meant to imply intimacy, but this effect is diluted when used by everyone we meet. Vague terms of affection, such as 'darling' or 'mate', can be even more infuriating.

Some might argue that the decline in the use of titles reflects a more serious breakdown of respect in our society – but perhaps we should applaud the increasing lack of empty formalities. Surely it is better to have agreeable manners and call someone by their first name, than be rude to someone while rigidly adhering to the correct form of address?

*See also Informality; Titles*

## FLAKING

A tendency to flake (or flake out) is a very modern affliction, meaning the habit of cancelling plans, often at late notice, for no good reason.

A social engagement always seems more appealing when it's two weeks away than it does on the afternoon of the same day, but it's important to resist any natural tendency towards inactivity and reclusiveness.

You might feel daunted by the prospect of a birthday gathering at which you know no one but the host, but you will almost certainly have a better time than you expect. The friendship points you garner will also pay dividends when it's your turn to sit nervously in the pub, hoping that someone will show up to help you drink that pre-emptive bottle of birthday prosecco.

As a repeat-cancelling offender, on the other hand, you may become known as a flake, remembered more for being unreliable than for any social contribution you make.

Almost as bad are those who frequently decline invitations. Saying no from the outset is marginally preferable to accepting initially only to have a change of heart, but beware: if you consistently refuse invitations, they may stop being issued.

If you are the person who is being flaked upon – the flakee – look on the bright side of being blown out. Accept the cancellation gracefully, and don't punish the flake with a hurt response. Instead, savour that unexpected night in with no one to see and nothing to do.

## FLATMATES

Living with friends or acquaintances can be a huge amount of fun, but also brings with it plenty of potential for tension.

When you move in with new people, set the ground rules early on: how will bills be split? Are the milk and butter communal? How is the house going to stay clean and tidy? Consider a housework rota, or employ a cleaner.

Your bedroom is yours to treat as you wish – as long as no odours permeate its perimeter – but communal areas should be tidy and free from your belongings. Respect your flatmates' privacy; always ask before you borrow clothes or toiletries.

Long, hot baths or showers may result in strained relations, so keep an eye on the clock.

If you need to raise a particular issue with a flatmate, do so politely and in person, rather than resorting to passive-aggressive notes or group messages.

## FLATTERY

*'Flattery is all right as long as you don't inhale.'*
ADLAI STEVENSON

The key difference between flattery and compliments is that compliments are real, while flattery is fake.

Flattery still serves a social purpose, however. Assuring a friend that, yes, her diet has really worked when you know she's feeling low in the self-esteem stakes is kind. Flattering your boss that he or she is a great manager is purely common sense. Being flattered by your partner, whether alone or in front of others, brings a cosy glow for all.

But for flattery to work its inoffensive magic, the person being flattered must be fully aware of the nature of the spell: don't ever believe the propaganda.

*See also Compliments*

### FLIRTING

*'God created the flirt as soon as he made the fool.'*
VICTOR HUGO

There are two types of flirting: social and romantic. Social flirting helps the world go around. Successful social flirts put those around them at ease; they recognise the line between fun and creepiness.

Romantic flirting has a purpose. A background information check is essential – is your target single? (More to the point, are you?) Is your best friend also interested? A few secret smiles and some careful eye contact (no staring) is a good starting point.

Conversation should be kept fun and light – some gently teasing banter helps to create rapport, but don't stray into personal remarks that could offend. Be wary of attempting physical contact, however innocent, unless it is initiated by the other person.

Above all, flirting is about being appropriate and knowing when to stop and move on. Never flirt with your best friend's other half, or your partner's best friend/brother/sister/mother/father.

## FLOWERS

Flowers are incredibly versatile. They are the perfect impromptu present, an appropriate gesture to acknowledge a very happy, special or sad occasion, and they can seal the deal when trying to impress. If you have let someone down or fear you have caused offence, flowers may say more than an embarrassed apology.

Be prepared to spend, and don't economise. Never buy bunches that look as if they might expire the following day. Don't overlook the importance of the card that accompanies a delivered bouquet – it is an important part of the present.

Make sure the bouquet suits the occasion and the style of the recipient. Avoid white flowers for celebratory bunches (they are often associated with funerals and death), and be careful with overwhelming scent, which can trigger allergies.

Local, seasonal blooms will usually be better value and often last longer.

## FOOD, PHOTOGRAPHING

A beautifully presented dish might cry out to be photographed, but while some chefs will consider it a compliment (and appreciate the extra publicity if you share the picture online), others will lament the presence of camera phones in their restaurant.

If you must photograph your food in a restaurant, be as unobtrusive as possible: make sure the flash is switched off and don't agonise over angles and shadows, preventing fellow diners from making a start on their meals.

## FOREIGN OBJECTS IN FOOD

You may be unlucky enough to find a hair in your soup, a slug in your salad, or even something completely unidentifiable in your meal.

If you are in a restaurant, alert the waiter or manager, who should be happy to change it.

If you are eating at someone's house, play it down and leave the object on the side of your plate or concealed in a napkin; your friend will feel bad enough without you making things worse.

If you unknowingly put the foreign object in your mouth, remove it discreetly by bringing your fork to your mouth, placing the offending item on it and lowering it to the side of your plate.

## FOREIGN TRAVEL

It's important to abide by foreign customs while travelling, but developing an understanding of these can be tricky. Whether it's showing the soles of your feet in Thailand, leaning up against a Maori table in New

Zealand or eating with your left hand in India, the
pitfalls are numerous.

The best place to start is some basic research: ask your
host or the hotel at which you are staying or consult a
friend who has visited your chosen destination. Search
online and read that boring bit at the beginning of the
guide book about customs and etiquette.

Err on the side of caution when it comes to revealing
clothing, and keep your eyes peeled for how those
around you are behaving. If the monks around you are
silent when you visit a Buddhist temple, follow their lead
– or, at the other end of the politeness spectrum, if
you're trying to get bus tickets at a bus station, don't
waste time queuing politely in a line if the locals are
scrummaging in a free-for-all.

Don't assume that everyone on your travels speaks
English – or should do. A good starting-point is to have
some humility about your own inability to speak
anything in their language beyond 'How much is this?'

If you're travelling with others, bear in mind that
overseas travel with even your closest friend can place
unexpected strains on the relationship. These can be
avoided if you adhere scrupulously to the usual rules of
living together. Little things – like keeping yourself clean,
sticking to joint arrangements, making sure you're as
punctual as possible, adhering to an agreed budget, and
trying to remain calm in the face of unexpected changes
in plan – can all help to ease your travelling experience.

## FORGETTING NAMES

*'Men are men; the best sometimes forget.'*
WILLIAM SHAKESPEARE

Remembering the names of people to whom you have been introduced can be a haphazard business. Some names are unusual to the point of absurdity, and will therefore stick in your mind. Others are instantly forgettable, and drastic measures need to be taken.

Using the name a couple of times in conversation soon after you've first heard it might fix it in your memory (but don't overdo this, or you'll sound like an importunate salesman).

Try visualisation techniques. For example, as soon as you hear the name, mentally blazon it across the person's forehead.

Or try a mnemonic; think of something memorable that rhymes with the name. Don't become so obsessed with remembering the name that you fail to participate in the conversation, however.

If you do forget, don't panic — you can generally negotiate your way through a conversation without naming names, and you can always find out later. If all else fails, a charming and self-deprecating 'I'm so sorry, I'm terrible at remembering names, I always do this …' should ensure that you don't offend anyone.

*See also Introductions*

*'Friends help you move. Real friends help you move bodies'.*
MILTON BERLE

The advice on how to be a good friend could be summed up in one word: listen. Your job as a friend is to be there when needed, at all times and in all scenarios.

It is useful to understand both the passive and active parts that go into the high-octane cocktail of true amity. Passively, you listen, comfort, support; you know not to give direct advice but merely reflect back a slightly tweaked version of their own view. You always turn up at their birthday parties, bail them out of boring situations at other people's parties, you act as alibi or frontman in complicated situations, you are unstinting in your generosity in lending clothes, money and time. You resist the inevitable envy when your friend surpasses you on the love, career, and looks front.

True friendship often requires action and intervention, however. A true friend knows when to say something that no one else can (whether it's about their bad behaviour or their bad taste); you can anticipate their needs without them having to ask for your help every time; you positively avoid flirting with their partner. Sometimes you will have to be a good friend even when you don't quite agree with the friend's point of view.

You may fall out with your friend, but you will manage this so that it's a good clean blowout,

not a festering boil of resentment that is far more
painful to lance.

Never make the mistake of merely neglecting a good
friendship; no matter how tried and tested, it is still a
plant that needs watering. We are probably ruder to our
good friends than to anyone else: social niceties are
deemed superfluous, but friendships can be surpris-
ingly fragile.

If you are obeying all these strictures, the least you can
expect is the same in return. Sometimes, the hardest
thing is recognising that a friendship is not truly
reciprocal, and ending it.

*See also Overfamiliarity*

## FUNERALS

Depending on the age and circumstances of the deceased
and the wishes of their relatives, a funeral can either be a
very sad occasion or a fond celebration of a life. Those
who issue the invitation will usually give you an
indication of what to expect.

A funeral service is open to the public, unless the
family of the deceased request that it be a private
ceremony. When attending a funeral, dress sombrely
unless an alternative dress code has been stipulated.

Men should wear a dark suit with a white shirt and
dark tie. Women might choose not to wear black, but
should opt for similarly subdued colours and simple,

clean lines. If a hat is worn, it should not be too eye-catching. Dress with an eye to the weather, remembering that churches and cemeteries can be cold, even in the height of summer.

The practical elements of a funeral can vary according to local tradition and the family's wishes. Often the mourners take their place in the church before the coffin is brought in, which is followed by close family. In a crematorium, the mourners may follow the family into the building, after the coffin. Whatever the venue, the front right-hand seats are reserved for the family, with the chief mourner sitting on the end of the front row, nearest the coffin.

Follow requests regarding funeral flowers carefully – many families specify that flowers should not be sent, or that a charitable donation is preferred. Where flowers are appropriate, choose a tasteful spray or a wreath. Pure white is considered the most fitting colour, though sending particular flowers that are known to have been a favourite of the deceased is a touching personal gesture. The accompanying card should be addressed to the deceased, not the family, and should bear a message of memorial, not of sympathy. The classic message reads 'In loving memory'. Flowers should be sent directly to the undertaker.

GARLIC TO
GYM ETIQUETTE

## GARLIC

Consider those around you when it comes to garlic. If you're cooking for others, be careful not to overpower the food with garlic — it is a strong taste, which your guests may not share. If you are going to be in close contact with others after eating garlic, bear in mind that they will be able to smell it on your breath, even if you can't.

## GHOSTING

Ghosting somebody means disappearing from their life by ceasing all contact and ignoring their attempts to contact you.

Ghosting is particularly common in fledgling romances, but it has been known to happen in longer-term relationships and friendships too.

It goes without saying that there is no excuse for ghosting — it's lazy and cruel, and if you ever bump into a person you once ghosted, the encounter is likely to be supremely awkward.

If you don't wish to see somebody again, simply tell them so: the initial sting of rejection is far preferable to that person having to endure weeks of uncertainty over the relationship, speculating about what they might have done wrong, or even fearing that you've been mown down by a bus without their knowledge.
*See also Ending a Relationship*

## GIFS

Amusing, short animations – often featuring well-known film or cartoon characters – gifs are popular on social media and in instant messaging, acting as a witty shorthand to express a reaction or opinion.

Don't overdo your use of gifs or the joke will start to wear thin. Only ever send a gif to somebody you're sure will receive it in good humour. If you send a 'crying' gif in response to bad news, for example, you risk coming across as sarcastic or passive-aggressive.

## GODPARENTS

A child traditionally has three godparents: a boy has two godfathers and one godmother, and a girl has two godmothers and one godfather. A godparent's first role will usually be to attend the christening or other religious or non-religious ceremony such as a naming ceremony. They may be called upon to make certain promises in keeping with their role.

Tradition also dictates that a godparent is expected to become the legal guardian of the child should anything happen to the parents, but this scenario is unlikely today. If this is the intention, the parents should make a formal statement of it in their wills.

Careful thought should go into both choosing godparents and considering whether to accept the role.

Being asked to be a child's godparent is a huge honour. Before accepting, ask yourself honestly whether you are prepared and able to fulfill the role. Try to understand what the parents want from you. You must be ready and willing to have regular contact with the family: don't enter into this relationship knowing that you will be one of those godparents whom no one has seen for years.

As godparent, you can be in the gratifying position of being the child's first grown-up friend and confidant. Treat them as your equal, and never judge or nag your godchild. Make yourself accessible; when they're old enough, give the child your mobile number or email address and let them know that they can always contact you for a chat.

Never forget a birthday or Christmas. Send postcards from holidays and let them know that they are in your thoughts.

*See also Christenings*

## GOOGLE

Google has become our first recourse for resolving any number of queries: journey time, unfamiliar symptoms, spellings – or the name of the catchy song on an advertisement.

If you Google somebody before meeting them, take whatever information you glean with a pinch of salt:

don't let a smug Twitter bio put you off the real person.

In a professional context, limit your Googling to professional platforms such as company websites and LinkedIn: if you snoop on a new contact's Instagram feed, you risk revealing your nosiness by asking after the matcha latte they enjoyed that morning when you meet face-to-face.

Don't allow Google to become an impediment to curiosity, and remember that a certain amount of ignorance is no bad thing. Responding to an enquiry with, 'that's an excellent question and I really don't know' will make you seem more open and approachable than immediately whipping out your phone to track down the official answer.

## GOSSIP

*'It is perfectly monstrous the way people go about nowadays, saying things against one, behind one's back, that are absolutely and entirely true.'*
OSCAR WILDE

Humans are predisposed to gossip: we know we shouldn't repeat scandalous stories, pass on personal anecdotes to a wider audience, or take public enjoyment from someone else's misfortunes, but we also know that not all gossip is toxic.

We owe much of our knowledge of our human history

to the written gossip of correspondents down the millennia. Gossip is an important information exchange, a way of defining what is (and isn't) socially acceptable. It often serves as a useful vent for anger that might otherwise erupt into real conflict.

Part of the fun of gossip lies in the danger; being overheard is a real risk, so watch your back. If you realise that you've been overheard spilling secrets, or accidentally send a gossipy text message to the subject of that message, you can either apologise or try to bluff it out and pretend you never knew it was top-secret material.

If you overhear some gossip about yourself, it is tempting to let the guilty parties rant on before letting them know you heard everything. Avoid this temptation: either remove yourself from earshot or confront the offenders on the spot.

*See also Whispering*

## GRAMMAR

In an age when instant communication is key, and text messages and emails are littered with abbreviations and verbless sentences, it seems impossibly old-fashioned to insist on good grammar.

But even in a world of immediate messaging, grammar is important because it clarifies thought and removes ambiguity. If you want to be understood, take time to

think about punctuation, verb agreement, syntax and spelling — recipients will appreciate the clarity of your writing. In extreme scenarios, poor grammar can signify the opposite of what you intend it to — you might be inadvertently agreeing to something because you put a comma in the wrong place.

Use spell-checkers discriminatingly; they are not 100 per cent reliable, as they do not check the context in which you use the words. Remember: no one was ever lampooned for writing well.

## GREETING CARDS

Greeting cards can be used for a multiplicity of occasions, from birthdays to congratulations to thank-yous.

It is usually preferable to write a personal letter of condolences or thanks for hospitality; alternatively you can write a message inside a blank card.

If you choose a card with a customised greeting, ensure that it is appropriate to the occasion and the recipient — be especially careful around the more risqué messages.

Make sure you know your recipient well before choosing a humorous card — you might find a joke about old age hilarious, but you run the risk of offending the other person if they fail to see the funny side of turning 50.
*See also Christmas Cards*

## GUEST LIST

Those with friends in high places can fast-track
themselves to the other side of the velvet rope in a
nanosecond; if you are lucky enough to be on the list,
never make a song and dance about your elevated status.

If there's 'been a mistake' and your name is
mysteriously missing from the guest list, don't try the
'don't you know who I am' trick. Desperation is unlikely
to get you VIP treatment.

## GUESTS, HOUSE

Some people are the perfect house guests. They arrive on
time, bearing carefully-chosen gifts, regale you with
entertaining stories, wash up, make their own beds and
leave early in the morning. Others invite themselves,
come late (or early), only remember to warn you of their
food intolerances as you're putting plates of lovingly-
prepared food in front of them, drink your best wine,
bore on about their lives, and leave their room looking
like a bomb site.

The true house guest from hell, however, is the one that
does all of the above and then doesn't know when to leave.

As the expression goes, 'visitors, like fish, stink in
three days'. If you are the visitor, follow an easy code of
behaviour to avoid this eventuality.

Confirm both arrival and departure times well before

you're due to show up. Bring a present, not necessarily flashy, but thoughtful — for example, a single malt if you know it's their particular tipple.

Keep the physical evidence of your presence in their house to a minimum and tidy up after yourself. Above all, leave exactly when you said you would: too early and it looks like you're trying to escape, too late and you've outstayed your welcome. Once you're home, send a handwritten note thanking your hosts for their hospitality.

If you're the host, do your bit too — putting flowers into a tidy spare room with fresh sheets and not making too big a deal about cooking extra meals. Don't be a martyr, accept offers of help, and resist the urge to celebrate as soon as their car is out of sight — just in case they've forgotten their wellies and turn back …

*See also Visitors, Unexpected*

## GYM ETIQUETTE

Wear clean, presentable gym clothes and deodorant when working out. Carry a towel with you and try to keep sweat off the machines.

Wipe equipment down when you have finished with it. Don't hover over users mid-workout, silently urging them to hurry up and get off the equipment you want to use. Don't offer advice on other people's workouts and don't stare at fellow gym-goers.

If you're wearing headphones, keep your music at a volume inaudible to others, and ensure that others are not watching the TV before changing channels.

If you must take selfies or videos during your workout, make sure you're not capturing other unwitting gym-goers in the process.

HANDSHAKES TO
HYPOCHONDRIA

## HANDSHAKES

A firm handshake, lasting a few seconds, is the common form of greeting for all business situations and most social situations too. Always use your right hand, and 'pump' the hand two or three times before you let it go. Ensure that your fingers grip the other person's palm, otherwise you will crush their fingers. Be careful not to grip too tightly, but do not offer a limp hand either. Check that your palms are not sweaty or clammy before shaking hands.

Be aware that in some situations, a handshake is not appropriate. Muslim men and women do not shake hands; instead, the man will place his hand, palm down, just above his heart and slightly bow his head in greeting.

Bowing is the traditional form of greeting in many East Asian countries, but handshakes are widely used and accepted, especially in business scenarios.

## HANDWRITTEN

*'Poets don't draw. They unravel their handwriting and then tie it up again, but differently.'*
JEAN COCTEAU

Just like the demise of the book, the death of handwriting should not be assumed. Emails, texting and even phone calls fade into white noise beside the elegant, deliberated simplicity of the handwritten note.

Nothing quite compares to the appeal of crisp vellum

stationery and the elegant flow of letters pouring across a page. Yes, we now have the printed word, but do we want future generations to believe that ours was an age of bank statements and bureaucracy?

Where are the love letters, the tellings-off from parent to teenager, the little *billets-doux* of correspondence that used to be intrinsic to everyday life? Stored on servers, listened to by bugging governments, deleted from voicemails?

Handwriting may still be taught at school, but for how much longer? As children grow older, homework is increasingly typed up and submitted by email. Unless children are encouraged to treat handwriting as a useful skill, we face the danger of generations who are only able to touch-type, cut and paste.

Make a stand by putting pen to paper occasionally. Handwritten notes are both personal and permanent; postcards survive to amuse well beyond the first 'Wish you were here' impulse, and a love letter is worth a thousand texts.

*See also Email*

## HASHTAGS

When used effectively, hashtags can highlight a particular issue, launch a campaign, or attract a new audience to the content you share on social media. Try not to be cynical in the way you use them, however — they should accurately reflect the content of your post rather than being used purely to garner likes or followers. Tagging an advertisement for your accountancy business with #KittensofInstagram is disingenuous and likely to cause frustration.

Hashtags can also be useful for pooling and sharing photographs from an event – #BrownJonesWedding, for example. If you decide to allocate a hashtag to your nuptials, birthday party or charity event, do so with a tongue-in-cheek attitude and keep it low key. Insisting that all your guests live-stream photographs of your #WeddingoftheCentury will most likely cause confusion and chaos, and will prevent them from participating fully in the occasion.

## HATS

Hats are worn both informally – beanies, flat caps, berets and baseball caps – and for certain formal events.

Women are required to wear a hat to the enclosures at Royal Ascot and some other smart race meetings. Hats are also traditional, but by no means compulsory, at weddings, and a matter of personal choice for christenings or funerals.

It is notoriously difficult to kiss socially while wearing a wide-brimmed hat. There is a knack to tilting the head at a suitable angle, but two women both in wide-brimmed hats should avoid such an 'intimate' greeting.

Nowadays, men rarely wear hats except for morning dress, when grey felt or the less usual black silk top hats are worn. They should be worn on the front of the head or carried under the arm, but should not be worn indoors or in formal photographs.

For the Royal Enclosure at Ascot, however, they are obligatory and must be worn at all times. 'Doffing' a top hat – raising it above the head to greet guests – shows a certain degree of panache.

*See also Morning Dress; Weddings*

## HANGOVERS

*'Always do sober what you said you'd do drunk. That will teach you to keep your mouth shut.'*
ERNEST HEMINGWAY

Hangovers are generally self-inflicted, so you should approach the day after an evening's overindulgence with stoicism and keep your misery to yourself.

Employers will not be impressed with employees who turn up for work feeling the after-effects of a night's boozing, especially if it interferes with standards of work. Make sure you arrive at work on time, keep your head down, drink plenty of water and coffee, and don't tell everyone how many shots you enjoyed (or are regretting) the night before.

Classic hangover cures range from a fry-up or bacon sandwich, to a Bloody Mary or other tried and tested

'hair of the dog' remedies. Of course, there is always the option of mitigating the effects of the alcohol: drink plenty of water, make sure you eat, and call it a day before you're thrown out.

## HEADPHONES

Tinny music emanating from headphones is an everyday hazard, especially on public transport. If you are using headphones, be aware that your music – distorted, percussive, maddening – may be painfully audible to your next-door neighbour, and adjust the volume accordingly.

But, for all their failings, headphones should always be used. It is the height of bad manners to inflict music, or a noisy film or TV soundtrack, on other people in a confined public place.

## HICCUPS

Inherently comic (especially when tipsy), but deeply irritating, hiccups are involuntary and, arguably, should need no apology. Such an intrusive noise should definitely be acknowledged, however – 'Excuse me, I seem to have the hiccups' should cover it (no need to apologise every time).

If the attack goes on for a long time, and is becoming an annoying distraction, it might be best to withdraw to the bathroom, where you can experiment with a range of

home remedies (holding breath, drinking from wrong side of cup, doing handstands etc.) in private.

## HOMESHARING

Whether you're sofa-surfing with friends or using a homesharing service for holiday accommodation, remember that you're effectively a guest in someone else's home, and treat it with due care.

Leave the house or apartment tidy and clean, and keep noise to a minimum during your stay so as not to annoy the neighbours. Follow any instructions about alarms, keys and security systems.

Don't be tempted to nose into any private areas or rifle through your host's belongings. If you're staying with children, try to avoid spillages or breakages, and prevent them from jumping on beds or furniture.

## HONESTY

*'It is always the best policy to speak the truth, unless of course you are an exceptionally good liar.'*
JEROME K. JEROME

From a moral standpoint, honesty is always the best policy. Honesty is good; we live in a complicated world already, so why muddy the waters even more with murky lies? But as anyone who has ever blurted out an unacceptable truth knows, honesty can hurt. So is it better manners to be honest and hurt someone, or to be dishonest and spare their feelings?

All too often, honesty is a cloak for cruelty. Any sentence that starts with the phrase, 'To be honest ...' is going to be a sentence in which the speaker will hurt the listener's feelings or self-esteem.

Children are often cited as being admirably honest, but if adults were to follow suit, we would all be miserable. Marriages would founder over the smallest issues; politics would grind to a halt; industries would collapse. Honesty is now an elusive luxury: it is an upstanding moral value that should be revered and placed on a pedestal. Down here in real life, a little dishonesty is a far kinder thing.

## HOSTING

*'When hospitality becomes an art it loses its very soul.'*
MAX BEERBOHM

Hosting a social occasion is both a pleasure and a responsibility. For all but the most impromptu gathering, some careful planning will enable both you and your guests to relax.

Check in advance that arrangements are clear. Your guests must know where you expect them to be, and when, including any directions and your telephone number in case of mishaps. Be clear about dress codes. If you would like guests to depart by a certain time, say so politely.

If you are serving food, recognise the limits of your culinary prowess and inclination. Your guests would rather enjoy your company over simple fare than attempt a fragmented conversation with you dashing frantically in and out of the kitchen.

Don't let yourself be monopolised: you may be the only person that some guests know, so be sure to circulate and make introductions where helpful. Be generous but not pushy with food and drink, and ensure that conversation is flowing.

As a guest, you should respond punctually to invitations; this will assist your host in making his or her plans. A prompt arrival, gracious demeanour, timely departure and a note of thanks will ensure that you appear on the guest list again, and a reciprocal invitation should follow where appropriate.

*See also Dinner Parties; Parties*

## HOTELS

On arrival at a hotel, ensure that you are happy with the room's location and standard: now is the time to negotiate improvements. Courtesy and a smile should ensure that you receive good service. Issues should be taken up with reception; only resort to speaking to the manager if you reach stalemate. If running late when checking out, a call to reception should secure an extra hour or two.

Don't help yourself to bathrobes, fixtures and fittings. On an extended hotel stay, ensure that the maid doesn't change linen every day – instructions are usually given in the bathroom or on the bed. Leaving used towels on the floor or in the bath is an invitation to have fresh ones substituted.

In smarter hotels, tipping will be expected. Give a small gratuity (i.e. one or two pounds, euros, dollars, etc., as appropriate) to bellboys or porters per piece of luggage if they take your bags to your room. Doormen should be tipped upon checking in and out if they have helped with taxis or luggage. A banknote may be left in your room for housekeeping. Check whether a service charge is included in your room service bill. If not, add ten per cent at the end of your stay and ask that it be given to the appropriate staff members.

Note that in some cultures, tipping is not expected, but may be appreciated. Japan is a notable exception where tipping is seen as excessive or possibly even rude: the Japanese consider excellent service to be part of their job. *See also Tipping; Valet Parking*

## HOUSEWARMINGS

When the stressful experience of moving home is over, and the dust has settled, what better way to relax and celebrate than with a housewarming party? Don't wait until your new home is a model of pristine, newly-decorated perfection; it's often a good idea to invite guests before you start the gutting and renovation process — it doesn't matter if they make a mess and spill red wine on your (soon to be discarded) carpets.

Housewarmings are also an excellent way of meeting people who live nearby, and give you an opportunity to glean some local intelligence about schools, shops, tradesmen, neighbours from hell, and so on.

If your good friend invites you to a housewarming it's a nice gesture (but not obligatory) to buy them something for their new home — glasses, ceramics, tableware or house plants are all good choices.

## HUMBLEBRAGGING

Worse even than the insult disguised as a compliment is the boast disguised as self-effacement: 'Another invitation from the Palace and I have literally nothing to wear!'

The humblebrag is part of the pervasive trend towards shameless self-promotion on social media — the implausible yoga pose, the adorable child, the nutritious homemade salad. Don't be fooled into thinking it's acceptable just because everybody else is doing it.

While success alienates, failure unites. If you must share personal updates with your social networks, make sure they are genuinely humble: you'll garner more respect for revealing that you've walked around all morning with your flies undone than you will for your sub-four-hour marathon time.

## HUMOUR

*'Humor is emotional chaos remembered in tranquility.'*
JAMES THURBER

Whether you're dealing with a train strike, a screaming infant or a senile parent, a sense of humour is one of life's essential tools. The most boring job can become tolerable if you can laugh with your colleagues about your boss's peculiarities.

Even tragedies can become bearable if one can apply some gallows humour – 'At least the house burning down means that we've finally got rid of that terrible wallpaper'.

The trouble is that imposing your own sense of humour on others can be perilous – snorting at an involuntary innuendo during a eulogy may be your way of coping with your grief, but it could well offend the bereaved family at a funeral. Regaling a dinner party with a rude story that you find utterly hilarious may not take into account others' more delicate sensibilities.

Remember that if you are proud of your sense of humour, you need to be able to laugh at yourself: don't fall into the trap of thinking that everything is funny as long as it is happening to somebody else.
*See also Jokes; Teasing*

## HUNGER

*'No clock is more regular than the belly.'*
FRANÇOIS RABELAIS

If hunger is making you 'hangry', control your temper and ensure that you eat sooner rather than later. Don't forget your table manners when you're hungry. There's no excuse for wolfing down your food without stopping for breath.

When you have finished your meal, it is bad form to announce, 'I'm stuffed' or even 'I'm full'. If somebody offers you second helpings, a more polite way of responding is simply, 'That was delicious, but I couldn't, thank you.'

## HYGIENE, PERSONAL

Personal hygiene need never become an issue if you pay attention to a simple regular routine: daily showers/ baths, frequent changes of clothing, use of deodorant, nail cleaning, and so on. If you're faced with a friend or colleague whose personal hygiene is questionable, try to address the issue directly (no anonymous 'gifts' of deodorant). Do it discreetly, and sympathetically, and make it clear that you're trying to help, not to embarrass.

## HYPOCHONDRIA

Hypochondria is a widespread ailment of the modern age; everywhere we look there are chronic malingerers who think that every spot is a rash, every sniffle 'flu, and every gasp their last. It's also infectious; competitive hypochondria can be a terrifying epidemic unless controlled.

Hypochondria — with its anti-social symptoms of being work-shy, self-obsessed and, at worst, self-righteous about your needs as an invalid — accounts for millions of working hours being lost every year. But hypochondria is just so tempting. In this callous world we live in, it's no good expecting any sympathy for anything less than a full-blown medical condition so you might as well exaggerate just to get some attention.

So go right ahead and moan to yourself that you're sure that cough is turning into pneumonia, just don't breathe a word to those around: they don't want your germs, imaginary or otherwise.

*See also Illness, Discussing*

ILLNESS, DISCUSSING TO
INVITATIONS, WEDDING

## ILLNESS, DISCUSSING

Everyone has days when they're full of cold or suffering from aches and pains. Try to remember that these are personal inconveniences, and should as far as possible be kept to yourself. Discussion of symptoms can all too often mutate into whingeing or, even more of a cardinal sin, over-explicit accounts of your symptoms. You should never be guilty of telling people things they really don't want to know.

If you're suffering from something very contagious or illness impairs your ability to work, be as honest as discretion allows and take the day off. Soldiering on may seem brave, but is often simply stupid.

*See also Bodily Functions; Hypochondria*

## INFORMALITY

The days when men referred to each other by their surnames and when office hierarchies were calibrated by the use of the prefix 'Mr' or 'Miss' are long gone. Informality is the order of the day; even in professional situations, when dealing with doctors, lawyers, policemen, bank managers, first names are being adopted.

There is much to be applauded here – empty conventions are often alienating and can impede communication. On the other hand, traditional fail-safes are very useful when you find it difficult to judge the social climate. If in doubt, opt for formality, and beware: older people may find the instant adoption of the first name disconcertingly overfamiliar.

*See also First Names, Use of*


## IN-LAWS

You know you're the luckiest person alive to have landed your perfect partner but when it comes to their relations, the laws of probability are not on your side. You've upset the balance of their family. At best you've swelled their ranks, further dividing the pot of love and attention. At worst you're the interloper, stealing their beloved son/daughter/brother/sister.

Even wonderful in-laws can create problems. If they're warm, uncritical, unfailingly supportive, always pleased to see you and hands-on with their grandchildren, this could expose cracks in your relationship with your own less-than-perfect parents or siblings.

Treat a bad in-law as you would the chickenpox. You don't want it, you don't deserve it, you can't really do much to alleviate it, but it's a necessary evil and if you stay calm and are careful not to aggravate it, you'll come out barely scarred. Sit tight, behave immaculately and trust that there will be no doubt between you and your partner about which family is the better bet.

## INSULTS, HOW TO RECEIVE

The challenge is to respond to insults in a way that
maintains the moral high ground; don't allow yourself to
be dragged down to the insulter's level. Contain your
anger and don't snap back with an immediate, aggressive
response — you may say things you don't mean.

Contemplate the insult in tranquility: consider the
possibility that you may have exaggerated or
misinterpreted the insult. Was it said with hurtful
intentions, or was someone offering constructive
feedback? Consult other friends or witnesses and see
what they think; confront the (no doubt unpleasant)
idea that there may be some truth in what has been said.

If you still feel the need to respond, do so in a calm
and measured way — no emotion or intemperate
language. Keep your response pithy and concise, and
don't return the insult or you will rapidly become
embroiled in an ongoing conflict.

## INTERNET DATING

With every romantic preference and predilection now
catered for online, internet dating gives single people
the ability to search for, and communicate with,
potential matches without having to run the social
gauntlet of the bar or club.

The love-by-design premise of the virtual world

might lack some of the romance of traditional courtship, but dating apps and sites open up a world of possibility that was previously unavailable.

If you're looking for a fellow dog-lover who also enjoys abseiling and Portuguese cinema, you can probably find them online, but being too specific in your demands may mean you miss out on your perfect match.

Honesty is always the best policy. Being 'creative' with photographs or profiles will only lead to disappointment when you meet in the flesh. Do use the best photograph you have, however: if the picture isn't up to scratch, potential lovers won't even bother reading the profile.

It's a competitive world online, and to succeed, you have to sell yourself. When you're writing your profile, steer clear of clichés and innuendo, aim for wit without sarcasm, and avoid excessive modesty or negativity.

Keep initial approaches brief and light-hearted. It's rude to ignore messages altogether, so a brief response, even if you're not interested, is always appropriate. Not everyone will abide by this rule, though, so if you are the one being ignored, give up graciously after two messages are left unanswered.

After you've exchanged a few messages, one of you needs to take the leap of faith and suggest meeting in person. When meeting someone for the first time, choose a public place and make sure that you've told a friend or family member where you're going.

## INTERRUPTING

Breaking into other people's conversation, stopping someone mid-flow, or finishing their sentences for them will make you appear impatient and overbearing.

If it is essential that you break into a conversation – to relay some important news or alert people to the fact that dinner is served, for example – establish eye contact with the person who is talking, and then say 'Please excuse me for interrupting, but ...'

## INTERVIEWS

Notorious for striking fear into the hearts of even the most confident, interviews are an opportunity for candidate and prospective employer to weigh each other up.

Immaculate presentation is essential, but gauge the formality of the company before dressing up in your best suit only to find that your interviewers are wearing jeans and t-shirts. Arrive on time, shake hands firmly, sit up straight and maintain eye contact. It's important to prepare, but remember that the interview is about you and not what you know about the organisation; select a few key facts to show you have done your research, and explain how your experience is relevant to the requirements of the job and why you want to work at that particular company.

Don't be afraid to enthuse about your achievements, but be honest and never name-drop. Ask questions; they provide a good opportunity for creating a more natural conversation and assessing the chemistry between you.

Thank the interviewer warmly. Whatever the outcome, your response should be gracious. Never burn bridges.

## INTOLERANCES, FOOD

Distinct from allergies or autoimmune conditions such as coeliac disease, food intolerances cause unpleasant symptoms such as bloating, stomach pain and nausea.

The reason behind a recent growth in food intolerances – particularly to dairy and gluten – remains unclear, but it has spawned a burgeoning market for 'free-from' foods such as oat milk and coconut flour.

If you're the one with the food intolerance, try to let your host know in advance of a social occasion rather than suffering in silence or leaving food untouched on your plate. Don't go into too much detail about your digestive tract or evangelise about the benefits of your newfound raw food diet.

Omnivores, meanwhile, should count themselves lucky and try to be tolerant of others' intolerances. If you're the host, make an effort to accommodate dietary requirements where possible: most supermarkets now offer substitute ranges so it's relatively easy to do so.
*See also Allergies*

## INTRODUCTIONS

*'Do you suppose I could buy back my introduction to you?'*
GROUCHO MARX

If you are the link between people who have never met, it
is up to you to make the introductions. Remember the
hierarchy: men should be introduced to women, junior
colleagues to senior ones.

Introduce individuals to the group first and then the
group to the individual. For example, 'Clare, this is
James, Daniel and Anna. Everyone, this is Clare.' Unless
the occasion is formal there's no need to mention
surnames. If possible, offering a little information
about each person as you introduce them ('Olly and I
were at school together') will help to break the ice. When
introduced, a friendly 'Hello, good to meet you' is the
standard response.

*See also Forgetting Names; Handshakes*

## INVITATIONS

The formality of an invitation should accord with that of
the occasion. More formal invitations are usually engraved
or printed on good quality card, about 6 x 4.5 inches (15 x
11.5 cm) in size, and should include the name of both the
host and hostess. The guest's name is handwritten on the
top left-hand corner. Any specific dress code (e.g. 'Black
Tie') and detail (e.g. 'Dancing 10 o'clock') may be stated.
Grown-up sons and daughters are usually sent separate

invitations, even when they live at home. However, when children's exact names, or their availability, are not known, it is permissible to add 'and Family' after their parents' names.

Equally, the addition 'and Guest' or 'and Partner' may be added – the reply should name the 'Guest' or 'Partner'.

*See also RSVPs or Debrett's Handbook for more information on the formatting and wording of invitations.*

## INVITATIONS, WEDDING

Wedding invitations nowadays come in all sorts of shapes and styles, but there is a traditional format: cream or white heavy card, folded, with the text usually in black copperplate script.

The traditional size of a wedding invitation is 8 x 6 inches (20.3 x 15.2 cm), folded in half, with the text on the first page. The name of the guest is handwritten in ink in the top left-hand corner. On formal invitations, guests should be addressed by their full title, for example, 'Mr and Mrs James Jones' or 'Miss Eleanor Sweet'. For less formal invitations it is acceptable to use only first names.

The traditional format for a wedding invitation where both parents are married (though many families will not fit into this pattern) is as follows:

*Mr and Mrs John Debrett request the pleasure of your company at the marriage of their daughter Charlotte to Mr Christopher Smith at The Church, Knightsbridge on Saturday 15th March 2009 at 3 o'clock and afterwards at The Hotel, London SW1*

The RSVP address is placed in the bottom left hand corner of the invitation.

Sometimes, guests are invited to only the wedding reception. A note, giving a good reason, should be placed inside the envelope, for example:

*Owing to the small size of St John's Church it is possible to ask only very few guests to the service. We hope you will forgive this invitation being to the reception only.*

Replies should be handwritten, in the third person, on headed paper. The envelope is addressed to the hostess and the date is written at the bottom of the page. For example:

*Mr and Mrs David Clegg thank Mr and Mrs John Debrett for the kind invitation to the marriage of their daughter, Charlotte, to Mr Christopher Smith at The Church, Knightsbridge, on Saturday 14th March 2009 at 3 o'clock and afterwards at The Hotel, and are delighted to accept (or: which they much regret being unable to accept).*

*See also Debrett's Wedding Handbook for more information on the formatting and wording of wedding invitations.*

JACKETS TO
JOKES

## JACKETS

A jacket worn with a shirt and tie and smart trousers is a standard interpretation of the stricter end of smart/casual, when an event does not require men to wear a suit. Equally, when a jacket is worn with smart jeans, a smart shirt but no tie, a man can be suitably dressed for the more relaxed end of the smart/casual spectrum.

There are a few places at which it is still compulsory for a man to wear a jacket. For example, the MCC Pavilion at Lord's, the Stewards' Enclosure at Henley, at certain private members' clubs, and in certain dining areas at The Ritz in London.

## JARGON

We all have 'issues' with jargon: let's all be proactive about the way we reach out, run it up the flagpole and kick the tyres, then come up with a value-proposition that really shows we're able to think outside the box … and so on.

The real problem with jargon is that it impedes communication and renders the simplest sentences opaque. It is frequently used to disguise ignorance, to wrong-foot colleagues and clients or to conceal ineptitude. It is anti-language and anti-communication.

If you are tempted to use jargon, think about why you are doing so. Do you actually know what you are trying to say? Can you understand yourself? Why are you using inverted commas around certain phrases? It is never a mistake to write, and speak, in plain, jargon-free English. You will be praised for the incisiveness of your thinking and rewarded for your ability to communicate clearly.

## JEALOUSY

*'Jealousy is the greatest of all evils and the one which arouses least pity in the person who causes it.'*
FRANÇOIS LA ROCHEFOUCAULD

Left untended, jealousy can be a blight on a perfectly good relationship. In some relationships, flirting with others and expressing admiration for someone else's beauty/charm/eligibility can pass without comment, relegated to the 'window-shopping only' category of behaviour. For other couples, such behaviour can breed real jealousy: but is it because one half is flirting too much or because the other half is over-reacting?

If your relationship is affected by jealousy, try the 'other shoes' test — imagine how you would react to your partner if they were behaving in the same way as you do, and vice versa.

The old-fashioned view was that a little jealousy was healthy to keep a relationship 'alive', but once unleashed, jealousy is challenging to manage. No one likes those conversations where one party is made to feel like a naughty school child and the other like a petulant brat.

Much better, then, to head jealousy off at the pass. If you see your partner flirting too much for your liking, neutralise it by joining in the conversation and endorsing the admiration, 'Yes, don't you have amazing eyes?' which will bemuse all concerned.

If you're the one flirting, and you see your partner starting to grimace, either extricate yourself gracefully and return to the nest or, if you still think they're over-reacting, smile and acknowledge them warmly and carry on with your harmless badinage.

Finally, jealousy often stems from insecurity, so you may need to ask yourself, or your jealous partner, exactly why you or they are feeling jealous ...

## JEANS

Jeans are a wardrobe stalwart, but they are still considered inappropriate for certain venues and occasions.

Don't wear jeans to a wedding, funeral, christening or other ceremony or important occasion. If you are mixing with the older generation, remember that denim may be frowned upon

Some bars and clubs, and nearly all members' clubs, have a 'no-denim' policy. Check ahead to avoid embarrassment.

*See also Smart Casual*

## JOKES

*'A difference of taste in jokes is a great strain on the affections.'*
T. S. ELIOT

Jokes are a serious business. Some of us imagine that jokes make the world go round — that dinner parties wouldn't be the same without them and that an opportunity to deliver a hilarious punchline should never be missed. We even have a day officially devoted to jokes: April Fools' Day. Jokes can also be an effective emotional release; post-disaster jokes are tasteless, tactless, cynical, exploitative ... and often horribly funny.

But the beauty of a joke is often lost on the beholder. Jokes can shrivel if they are misunderstood or greeted with a half-hearted chuckle in the name of 'politeness'.

A joke can also alienate or even cause offence, both in the joke-teller ('they just don't get my sense of humour') and in the audience ('actually, my wife is blonde and that's just rude'). Intuition and judgment are key.

Telling a joke can be a real conversation-stopper — if you're itching to relay the corker you heard earlier, appreciate that it will be disruptive, and tell it as quickly as possible before returning to real conversation.

The second rule is to match your material to your audience: a rude joke that had you and your friends crying with laughter is probably not one to tell your colleagues in the office.

*See also Humour; Teasing*

KEBABS TO
KNOW-ALLS

## KEBABS

Of Middle Eastern origin, kebabs come in numerous guises. In Western culture, the most familiar is probably the shish kebab, small cubes of meat and/or vegetables threaded on to a skewer. Remove the meat before eating by holding the skewer in your left hand and using the tines of a fork to ease the pieces, one at a time, on to your plate. Keep the tip of the skewer in contact with the plate for as long as possible to avoid the meat flying off in surprising directions, and never resort to using your fingers.

The doner kebab — thin slices of meat served in pitta bread with salad and sauce — has become, for many a hungry reveller, an essential staple to consume on the way home after a night out. If you succumb to kebab temptation, consider your transport options first: your taxi driver might refuse to pick you up if he or she spots a kebab in your hand. On a night bus or train it's highly anti-social to be tucking into a hot, meaty snack, however delicious. Either eat it beforehand or keep it wrapped up and save it for when you get home.

## KILLJOYS

People who trail a bad atmosphere, casting gloom over other people's enjoyment, are, quite literally, killjoys (also known as spoilsports, party-poopers or fun sponges).

It is alarmingly easy to become a killjoy: if you have had a bad day, or you are feeling tired and irritable, your mood can very easily infect those around you. If you are sour-faced and self-righteously intent on avoiding alcohol, and all around you are throwing caution to the wind, abstention can very quickly turn into disapproval.

Be aware of the effect you are having on other people: if your influence is baleful, then bale out.

## KILTS

There are two rules when it comes to kilts: they should only be worn by those with a Scottish or Gaelic connection, and the correct attire must be worn to suit the occasion.

Formal kiltwear involves donning one's own tartan – modern, ancient or dress. Ensure that the length of the kilt is right: whilst the contemporary trend is towards the shorter kilt, which sits above the knee, traditional wearers insist that it should sit high on the waist – beneath the bottom rib – and rest between the top and middle of the kneecap.

Accompaniments depend on the occasion. Daywear requires a plain tweed jacket, accompanied by plain sporran, shirt and tie, hose and brogues. The Prince Charlie or Kenmore doublet is appropriate for eveningwear. Marry this with a dress sporran, which is usually decorated with fur.

For a more versatile and less formal look, don an Argyll outfit: worn with a standard white shirt and classic tie, this attire is suitable for Burns Suppers, ceilidhs and afternoon weddings.

When asked what you are wearing under your kilt, an enigmatic smile will suffice.

## KINDNESS

*'Three things in human life are important. The first is to be kind. The second is to be kind. The third is to be kind.'*
HENRY JAMES

The foundation stone on which good manners rest, kindness is quite simply the ability to notice other people, recognise their needs or discomfort, and act upon that recognition.

Kindness requires an ability to empathise with others, and parents should encourage their children in empathy — kindness and good manners will naturally follow.

## KISSING, SOCIAL

Social kissing is a potential minefield and is usually dependent on situation, age, background, profession and your relationship.

As a general rule, don't kiss people you don't know. Don't kiss colleagues. Do kiss close friends and dates.

The key is to make your actions clear to avoid embarrassing confusion.

Usually it's right cheek first, but prepare to change direction at the last minute. Pull back decisively (but not abruptly) if you are just giving one kiss. Be cautious with those with whom you are less familiar — two might seem over the top. If confusion occurs over one-kiss-or-two, take charge and go in for a second.

It's not always as simple as one or two, however: the Dutch go in for three kisses, while in some parts of Northern France, four are insisted upon. However numerous they are, humour is useful in deflecting embarrassment over the meet-in-the-middle mix-up.

Don't air kiss, but there is a fine line between an acceptable peck and an overly affectionate smacker. Cheek skin must make brief, light contact; sound effects are unnecessary.

If you'd prefer to shake hands, be sure to hold yours out before any kissing manoeuvres begin but, if you're part of a group introduction, don't be the only non-kisser at the party.

*See also Introductions*

## KNOW-ALLS

We all know a know-all — someone who believes that they possess a superior intellect and wealth of knowledge, and who shows a determination to demonstrate that superiority at every opportunity. In a world where knowledge is power, the know-alls should be ruling the planet. Yet more often it seems to be that the more of a know-all someone is, the further they are from actually running things.

We all love trivia, useless knowledge and the occasional weird feats of memory, but most of us – the know-somethings – have the sense to realise that it is not clever to trumpet such empty expertise. On the contrary, the get-aheads often seem unencumbered by sacks of facts. While the know-alls are totting up the sum of their knowledge, the get-aheads are too busy getting ahead to sit and analyse whether they know quite a lot, enough, or all of it.

If you are faced with a know-all, pity them for their lack of self-awareness, listen intently to their trumpet-ings for the odd interesting fact and never, ever disagree with them, for that way leads to perdition and the perfect excuse for the know-all to pummel you with further 'incontrovertible' facts.

Then when you feel you've travelled as far as you can into the limitless vistas of the know-all's inner world, move on politely, leaving them, and their empty knowledge, behind you as you get on with real life.
*See also Mansplaining*

LAUGHTER TO
LYING

LAUGHTER

*'There is nothing in which people more betray their character than in what they laugh at.'*
JOHANN WOLFGANG VON GOETHE

The old saying, 'Laughter is the best medicine' has been proven to have some truth in it: studies have been conducted showing how people who can laugh at themselves and at life live longer and more happily. Laughter is aerobic and releases serotonin, which boosts your immunity, shoots pain-relieving endorphins around your bloodstream and even counters the effects of stress.

A little judgement should be exercised, however, before unleashing laughter indiscriminately. Laughing at a funeral is never acceptable, but laughing at the wake afterwards can be a life-affirming release. Laughing at a child's ear-piercing first attempts to play their recorder will never endear you to their proud parents; laughing at their stories of the little one's potty-training escapades will. It's all about prepositions – laughing *with* but not *at*.

Having a laugh with friends, family or loved-ones is what life is all about; laughing at someone else, or at someone else's expense, will lead to trouble. Stay clear of such trouble by being a generous chuckler, momentarily checking at what or whom your laughter is directed and remembering that laughter can also be cruel.

As for how one laughs – the sound of laughter is not universally tinkling and infectious, and can be downright grating. Ask a close friend for honest feedback on whether your laughter is charming or, frankly, frightening.

## LENDING

*'Neither a borrower nor a lender be,*
*For loan oft loses both itself and friend'*
WILLIAM SHAKESPEARE

Lending something to a friend should make us feel generous and bountiful, happy that we are able to help. In fact, what lending often does is taint that friendship and change its parameters. If a friend asks you to lend them something, they are effectively asking you how much you like and trust them. You are then placed in a difficult position. First, you secretly like them a little less for asking. Second, you can only say no for practical reasons (if you can't afford to lend them money, for example). Saying no for any other reasons effectively means that you don't trust them.

Before lending a valued possession, steel yourself to the likelihood that you may not get it back, and be upfront and unemotional about your Terms and Conditions:

'Yes, you can take that coat, but I need it by the weekend in a good enough state to wear at a wedding'.

It's more liberating to give something rather than to

lend it, if you possibly can. Then it is within your control to limit or expand the gift, squash the sense of obligation and move on.

*See also Borrowing*

## LETTER WRITING

*'Sir, more than kisses, letters mingle souls; for thus, friends absent speak.'*
JOHN DONNE

Always use quality stationery for correspondence, whether business or personal. Personal letters should be handwritten on paper that is robust enough to avoid show-through. Use a lined undersheet to keep text straight and use black or blue ink.

A personal letterhead should include postal address, telephone number and email address, but not your name. The envelope should match the writing paper and have a diamond flap. Always date personal correspondence. Don't frank pieces of personal correspondence – use a stamp.

Business letters should be typed on A4 paper that includes the company logo, postal address, telephone number and email address. If any of this information does not appear on pre-printed business letters, be sure to add the pertinent contact details yourself. Type the recipient's name and address at the top left-hand side of the letter.

The date goes beneath this, also on the left-hand side.

Every effort should be made to establish your recipient's name, but use 'Dear Sir/Madam' if you're not able to do so. If you are familiar with the recipient, use his or her first name only, e.g. 'Dear David'. If in doubt, follow how they have styled themselves in previous correspondence. Otherwise, opt for formality.

Add a 'subject line' after the salutation – centre and embolden/underline it. This will be useful for sorting, prioritising and filing. Aim not to exceed one sheet of paper – it goes without saying that brevity and precision are preferable in business correspondence.

The sign-off depends on the salutation. As a broad rule, if you addressed the letter to 'Dear Mr Townsend' the sign-off is 'Yours sincerely'. If addressed to 'Dear Sir/Madam', then 'Yours faithfully' is correct. 'Yours truly' is a less businesslike alternative to an acquaintance you don't know well.

## LETTERS AFTER NAMES

Use letters after your name appropriately. Writing your university degree after your name when writing to friends looks pretentious, but including appropriate professional letters on a business card makes sense.

No letters after the name should be added on invitations, but on formal lists and in professional correspondence they may be included.

*See also Debrett's Handbook for the order of precedence of letters after names.*

## LIFTS

In lifts, like all enclosed public spaces, there is an invisible boundary around people.

Generally, lifts command silence or hushed tones. Allow people out of the lift before you try to get in, and don't cram yourself in to crowded lifts; instead, wait for the next one.

If you are next to the control panel, you should take the responsibility for using it — politely select the correct floor for other people and hold the 'doors open' button if you spot someone dashing for the lift before it departs.
*See also Personal Space*

## LINKEDIN

LinkedIn is an online CV and recruitment platform and a useful tool for professional networking. Bear this in mind when setting up your profile: use a good quality photograph that looks professional rather than a group photo taken on a night out with friends. A fairly formal portrait shot, usually head and shoulders, is appropriate, ideally in business dress.

Connect only with people you have met in person or with whom you have corresponded at length by email. If necessary, add a personal note when you send the invitation, eg. 'Great to meet you at last week's event. Look forward to speaking again soon.'

Ensure you keep your LinkedIn profile up-to-date with any promotions or career moves. Engage with your news feed and share content that's relevant to your industry, but don't post any links to inflammatory or overly-political material.

Ask for recommendations or endorsements by approaching former and current colleagues with a personal message — emphasising the fact that you are simply updating your profile rather than looking for a new job. Ensure you reciprocate promptly and generously if and when necessary.

## LISTENING

*'The reason we have two ears and only one mouth is that we may listen the more and talk the less.'*
DIOGENES

Listening to a friend who is going through a divorce, has suffered a bereavement, or who has lost their job, is the most generous part of a friendship. It is generous because by listening, and listening again, and listening some more, you are stifling one of the keenest of human instincts, the need to respond. This is crucial.

Listening is not about waiting to say your bit. Listening is realising that nothing you can possibly say at that moment could help as much as allowing the other person to unburden themselves. You may or may not be asked for an opinion at some point in the crisis but, for now, listening is what you must do.

There is a skill in listening that goes beyond the ability to remember each detail for future reference (although this is important). Stay focused and nod and shake your head at appropriate moments — never let your eyes glaze over. Concentrate on what is being said and maintain eye contact; listening while glancing occasionally at your phone is obviously not good enough. Beyond an immediate crisis, listening attentively will serve you well in other fields.

Listening can often tell you far more than you merely hear — whether it's the latest gossip at work, your child confiding something important to you, or your aged parent casually mentioning a trip to the doctor.

## LOUNGE SUITS

Lounge suits are normal business suits, worn for semi-formal occasions with a shirt and tie. The equivalent for women is a skirt or trouser suit or sometimes a cocktail dress depending on the time of day and the occasion. If 'lounge suits' are stipulated on an invitation, it is fine to ask your host if you need a little more clarification.

*See also Smart Casual*

## LYING

*'Any fool can tell the truth — the best liar is he who makes the smallest amount of lying go the longest way.'*
SAMUEL BUTLER

Lying is an instinctive and unavoidable aspect of the human condition. We grow up to learn that we should not lie, that lying is a human vice and that telling lies will always get us into trouble in the end. Later on we also learn that lies are used on a multiplicity of occasions and come in all colours and all sizes: from irreproachable white to irredeemable black, via purple (embroidered truth), yellow (cowardly excuses) and grey (minor deceptions).

Ultimately, we realise that life is all the richer and more subtle for a few shimmering shades of truth.

How to be a good liar? In moral terms, lies that are told to be kind, or to spare hurt, will always triumph over lies that are told for their own sake, or to cover up wrongdoing.

Don't overdo the fabrication: a life that gradually descends into a tissue of lies is a fragile thing — and others will distrust every single thing you say. In practical terms, a liar must avoid telltale signs like blushing, nervous giggling or rapid blinking, and keep it simple. Stick to a bone of truth, merely fleshing it out with easily remembered exaggerations and logical extrapolations.

If you suspect somebody else of lying, there are three ways of dealing with it. You can ignore it: the lies are probably more to do with the insecurities and problems of the liar than they are to do with you. Or you can turn to forensic questioning, then sit back and watch them tie themselves in knots and struggle to remember each step. Finally, if they are a loved one or a good friend, you can stop them in their tracks and save embarrassment with a mild 'Come off it'.

Be careful when exposing lies, however, for they might herald the telling of uncomfortable truth. As Samuel Johnson said, 'A man had rather have a hundred lies told of him, than one truth which he does not wish should be told'.

*See also Honesty*

MA'AM TO
MORNING DRESS

## MA'AM

If you meet The Queen or other female member of the Royal Family for the first time, you should address them as 'Your Majesty' or 'Your Royal Highness', respectively.

From then on, use 'Ma'am', which should rhyme with 'jam'. In the Armed Forces junior officers also address female superiors as 'Ma'am'.

*See also Queen, HM The; Royal Family*


## MANSPLAINING

Mansplaining is the act of explaining a fact, process or procedure condescendingly and at great length to someone who is already well-versed in that particular subject. Despite its name, it is not just men who are guilty of mansplaining.

If you find yourself on the receiving end of a mansplanation, it can be entertaining to feign total, wide-eyed ignorance and let the other person drone on before correcting them on a point of obscure detail.

Alternatively, avoid the lecture altogether by interrupting the mansplainer as early as possible to say, 'Actually, I wrote my thesis on that particular case. Shall we move on?'

*See also Know-alls*

## MASSAGE

Don't let anxiety over spa etiquette come between you and the serious business of relaxing. Massage is all about creating the optimum conditions for tuning out, so always assert your preferences on background music, clothing, pressure and conversation. This is not the time for empty politeness; enduring discomfort defeats the object.

To prepare for your massage, you will usually be left to undress, lie down and cover up with a towel. Afterwards, you may be left alone again to regain consciousness. Don't feel obliged to leap up and grab your clothes – you will be prompted when your time is up.

Some employers now offer a roving masseur or masseuse to keep the troops supple, relaxed and productive. When indulging in the workplace, some decorum is required. If no private space is available, keep your shirt on and sound effects to a minimum.

## MATCHMAKING

*'Courtship is to marriage as a very witty prologue to a very dull play.'*
WILLIAM CONGREVE

Matchmaking can be a deeply satisfying activity, but just as with any other aspect of courtship, there is a ritual and a rhythm to ensuring it's a success.

To start with, you must be a shameless networker, so that by sheer number of potential matches, you can start to pair people up. Judge carefully whether you tell one, both or neither that they are being set up.

Never make the mistake of matching like with like too minutely – if the chosen two are too perfectly matched and similar, there might be no friction, and therefore no spark. Resist the temptation to manage the match; once the couple have been introduced and initial impressions fed back to the opposite party in judicial doses, the two should be left to get on with it.

If you yourself are being match-made, don't trust your parents; it is highly unlikely that you and they are looking for the same things in your prospective partner. If you allow yourself to be matched, don't then get annoyed with the match-maker when things don't work out: they are not responsible for the other person standing you up or failing to get in touch.

*See also Internet Dating*


## MEMES

An image, idea, catchphrase or activity that spreads rapidly amongst internet and social media users, a meme usually has little purpose other than as a kind of 'in-joke' or humorous diversion.

The viral impact of memes is unpredictable and difficult to replicate, but creating content that subsequently 'goes viral' is still regarded as the holy grail for marketing campaigns.

Share memes with caution, especially at work, and never share anything offensive or illegal. Be sure to acknowledge the original creator or photographer by tagging them in your repost.

## MILLENNIALS

Typically identified as those born between the early '80s and early '90s, Millennials are the children of baby boomers and also known as Generation Y. Having come of age with email and social media, they tend to be well-versed in digital communication.

Don't write Millennials off as shallow, vain and smartphone-obsessed, however. Research has shown that they are less likely to drink, smoke or take drugs than their elders, and are often more socially aware and tolerant. Let's not forget, too, that you'll probably need a Millennial's help to operate the printer at some point.

If you want to endear yourself to a Millennial, don't feel that you have to adopt his or her own language or mode of language: there's no need to sign up to Snapchat or to start using words like 'sick' and 'awesome'.

Be open-minded and interested in them, and resist the urge to impart too much of your worldly wisdom. Remember that the defining characteristic of a Millennial is that he or she knows more than you: you risk looking silly or naïve if you wade into the minefield of dating, relationships or career advice.

## MOBILE PHONES

Our phones have become our constant companions, able to communicate, take photos, play music, display the news and show films.

They are also capable of causing annoyance and offence, however, so remember that people in the flesh deserve more attention than your phone.

Put some distance between yourself and your phone in social situations: don't place it on the dining table or glance at it longingly mid-conversation. If you are awaiting an important call when meeting someone socially, explain at the outset that you will have to take the call, and apologise in advance.

If you answer your phone in a public place, ensure that your conversation is not disturbing other people. Don't use your phone in quiet zones on trains; elsewhere, be aware that your conversation will disturb a peaceful carriage of commuters. Intimate conversations are never appropriate in front of other people.

It's rude not to give people who are serving you your full attention, so end a call or finish writing a message before transacting other business – in banks, shops and so on.

When texting, using social media, reading or watching something on your phone, be aware that you will quickly become oblivious to your surroundings, so glance up now and again to check that there is nobody who needs help or to whom you should offer your seat. Avoid becoming engrossed in your phone when you're crossing roads or walking on pavements, or risk causing a collision.

Finally, switch your phone to silent when you are
going into meetings, theatres, libraries, the cinema or
the opera and keep the screen hidden: notifications
lighting up can be just as disruptive as sound.
*See also Quiet Zones; Text Messages; Voicemail*


## MONEY, DISCUSSING

The subject of money – whether our pay packets, our
debts or the value of our home – was long considered a
conversational taboo. It has become increasingly apparent, however, how much this coyness has led to inequali-
ty, with large salaries conferred arbitrarily on a few while
others with equal talents settle for considerably less.

If you think you deserve a pay rise, arrange a time to
speak to your boss and present your case unemotionally
and with supporting evidence (cost savings you've
realised or sales targets you've met). Remember that 'no'
doesn't necessarily mean no – be persistent and polite,
and ask what other options are available to you – a new
commission structure, performance-based bonus or
extra training in lieu of a pay rise.

Asking colleagues what they earn is a thornier arena, and
can cause resentment or discord at work. If you are seriously concerned, raise the issue with your HR department.

Outside of work, there is usually no need to discuss
money. There will always be Joneses to keep up with, but

bragging about your bonus or musing on your mortgage can make others feel inadequate and heightens the difference between your financial situation and that of the person you are talking to. Complaining about a shortage of money, however indirectly, is also likely to make the people around you feel guilty.

## MOOD SWINGS

We all have good days and bad days, and moods can vary according to an array of factors, from hunger levels to the weather. The important thing is to keep your fluctuating internal barometer strictly to yourself. No one wants to be subjected to your emotional highs and lows; your aim should be to project equanimity at all times.

If you do let your defences down and snap or lose your temper, apologise as soon as normality returns. Explain that you were temporarily deranged by hunger/insomnia/stress etc., and that your disconcerting behaviour was nothing personal.

*See also Hunger*

## MORNING DRESS

Morning dress (or 'formal day dress') is the traditional dress for weddings and formal daytime events in the presence of The Queen, such as Royal Ascot.

The morning coat has curved front edges sloping

back at the sides into long tails. It is single-breasted with one button, and usually has peaked lapels. Black or grey morning coats are nowadays considered equally acceptable.

Although grey is the traditional colour for a waistcoat under a black morning coat, patterned or coloured waistcoats are also acceptable. Brocade is a common choice, although silk might be more comfortable at a hot reception.

Single-breasted waistcoats should be worn with the bottom button undone. If the waistcoat is double breasted, all buttons should be fastened. Avoid backless waistcoats as you will not be able remove your morning coat.

Trousers should be grey with a grey morning coat, or grey and black striped (or grey houndstooth) with a black coat. Morning dress should be worn with a plain shirt (traditionally white with a stiff turned down detachable collar), although cream, pale blue or pink are equally acceptable. It should be double-cuffed, with appropriate cufflinks. The tie or cravat is traditionally of heavy woven silk. Black or silver is traditional, but non-garish pastels are frequently worn.

Formal black shoes should be laced up and highly polished, worn with black socks. Top hats are either grey felt — which are easier to come by — or black silk, which can be expensive. These are largely optional at weddings and should be carried rather than worn inside church.

For the Royal Enclosure at Ascot they are obligatory and must be worn at all times.

*See also Hats; Royal Ascot; Weddings, Attending*

# N

NAME-DROPPING
TO NUDITY

## NAME-DROPPING

The ever-so-casual dropping of a name into a conversation is usually a crude attempt to gain social kudos from someone else's reputation. If you really feel that name-dropping is necessary, do it subtly; never mention a name out of context, and only refer to people you really do know.

If you mention the names of people with whom you have only the most fleeting acquaintance you will be seen, rightly, as a delusional and needy celebrity stalker.

## NAPKINS

Napkins should be placed on the side plate or in the centre of the table setting, where the plate will go. They should be folded simply; avoid elaborate origami styles.

Before you start eating, unfold your napkin and place it on your lap. Never tuck it into the top of your shirt. Dab the corners of your mouth with your napkin if necessary during your meal, but do not make grand side-to-side wiping gestures. Never blow your nose on your napkin.

When you have finished eating, place your napkin, unfolded, beside your plate. If you are leaving the table temporarily, it can be left on your seat to indicate that you are returning.

*See also Table Manners*

## NAUGHTY STEP

A simple but effective form of mild punishment for young children, the naughty step — or equivalent chair, area or corner — is now widely deployed as a parenting technique. The idea that a particular place is sufficiently indicative of disgrace to prompt remorse and an apology is nothing new: in the past we might have sent someone to Coventry or banished them to an imaginary doghouse.

If your child misbehaves in front of others, it's fine to resort to your usual mode of punishment, but try to do so quietly and with minimum fuss. Never send another person's child to the naughty step unless he or she is a close family member and you are acting *in loco parentis*.

## NEIGHBOURS

*'There are two things we wish we could all live without: haemorrhoids and neighbours.'*
SPIKE MILLIGAN

Despite its idealistic associations, 'neighbour' is often a dirty word — particularly for city-dwellers. Proximity easily breeds contempt, and we can neither choose our neighbours nor exercise any control over their noise levels, pets, or attitude to parking.

Don't feel you have to turn adversarial, no matter how frustrating the late-night bass thumping through the walls or the floor. Litigation should be a last resort — try your best to negotiate any difficulties amicably first, and resist outright confrontation.

Neighbours need not just be a necessary evil. Make friends with your neighbours from the day you or they move in and enjoy the benefits. You can ask them to be key holders in case you get locked out, to take delivery of parcels for you, or to pop in and feed the cat if you're away.

If your children make friends with your neighbours' children, you can offload them for hours at a time. These arrangements are reciprocal, and you must be prepared to do the same for them, but just by enlisting them as friends, you will have joined the local community.

## NERVOUSNESS

*'I only drink to steady my nerves. Sometimes I'm so steady I don't move for months.'*
W.C. FIELDS

Nervousness is infectious. Try your best to hide the physical signs of nervousness – trembling hands, inappropriate giggling, jiggling feet, rapid speech – and you will find that being aware of, and controlling, the symptoms helps you to calm down.

Use good manners as a convenient shield to ease you through the more challenging social situations – reverting to accepted social norms will disguise nervousness. If you notice that someone is feeling nervous, deploy your best manners to put them at ease: asking simple, friendly questions will help to distract them from their anxiety.

## NOSE BLOWING

Sniffing loudly and repeatedly is inexcusable. Never be caught without a handkerchief or paper tissue. Most people have come to favour the latter, though carrying a clean, crisp cotton handkerchief is an outward sign of an organised life and will always impress.

Before blowing your nose, excuse yourself from company wherever possible. In reality, privacy is rarely an option and discretion is sufficient. The process should be silent and brief. Fold your handkerchief and dispose of it quickly.

Never use your hand – or your sleeve.

*See also Sniffing*

## NOSINESS

We all like to think we have an enquiring mind, rigorously questioning the world around us and trying to add to the sum of our knowledge every day. Yet there is clearly a fine line between acceptable curiosity and unacceptable nosiness. Are we being nosy if our enquiries take us beyond the need-to-know?

With a world of information now at our fingertips through search engines and social media, we can indulge our instinct for nosiness almost without limitation, but that doesn't mean it's right to do so.

Consult your conscience: if you are sleuthing for voyeuristic, non-educational reasons, then you're being nosy; if you are poking about because a situation might affect your life/decisions/dinner plans, fair enough.

Beware of accidentally exposing your nosiness: the inadvertent 'like' of an ex's four-month-old post, the letting slip in conversation of a personal detail garnered online.

In conversations with friends, a natural desire to be a confidante and offer well-informed comfort or advice can sometimes tip over into a voyeuristic salivation over gory details. If you sense your curiosity is making somebody uncomfortable, rein in the questions and let them do the talking.

## NUDITY

Some people would claim that nudity is a good thing; it's liberating, invigorating, just what nature intended. Others argue that nudity is disgusting: wobbly, hairy, mottled, chilly – and usually practised by the people who should, frankly, cover up. Which view do you hold?

Just as one covers up to show respect for certain religions and cultures, there is an element of 'when in

Rome' about accepting nudity on beaches in parts of Europe. Just consider whether your friends or family will ever forgive you if you follow (lack of) suit. Remember, too, that in this day and age there's a good chance of being photographed or videoed in the altogether by family, friends and strangers alike.

Even in the most naturist of environments, be sensitive to the feelings of others exposed to your nudity. Assess the climate in communal changing rooms: if nudity is prevalent, then it is wise to bare all – you don't want to look inhibited and body-shy by skulking into a cubicle. Similarly, if modesty prevails, don't strut around completely starkers.

As for nudity inside the house, basic rules of family decency apply, and remember that teenagers are particularly susceptible to shame.

When it comes to opening the door to visitors, signing for a package with your own on show will only embarrass the courier.

OFFICE PARTIES
TO OYSTERS

## OFFICE PARTIES

Behind the gloss of Christmas celebrations and the camaraderie of leaving dos is the reality that you are socialising with colleagues under the watchful eye of senior management. Be smart and social, but know when to draw the line. Circulate and socialise, but keep conversation upbeat and general. Don't be tempted to gossip or complain about your boss; instead focus on non-work-related subjects: families, children and holidays.

To avoid overdoing it on free alcohol, eat well, decline offers of shots, and alternate drinks with water. Have fun and enter into the spirit of the occasion, but don't be the casualty everyone is talking about (and sniggering at) the next day. If things start feeling dangerous, call it a night. If you spot a colleague who is looking worse for wear, remove them from any precarious conversations and get them into a taxi home.

The day after still counts too. Crawling in hungover and late (or worse, pulling a sickie) is unforgivably unprofessional.

## OFFICE POLITICS

Enforced proximity with our colleagues for eight or more hours a day creates a breeding ground for gossip, rivalry, friendship and romance, and few deskbound workers are spared the rollercoaster of the resulting

office politics. While some thrive on the drama, many simply endure it.

It is inevitable that you will be caught up in the politics of your office to some extent, but only participate in a way with which you feel comfortable. Be prepared to take the consequences of your actions if you become too involved.

When you encounter delicate situations with colleagues, handle them as sensitively as possible. If confrontation is necessary, be candid and unemotional, and then move on.

Idle gossip can be very damaging, and spreading it makes you look unprofessional, so abstain wherever possible. However immature or ruthless your colleagues may seem, remind yourself that they are human beings with lives outside the office. Treat all colleagues with courtesy, irrespective of hierarchy.

*See also Business Trips*

## OFFICE ROMANCE

*'He and I had an office so tiny that an inch smaller and it would have been adultery.'*
DOROTHY PARKER

The closeness and camaraderie of the workplace can often overflow into romance, but think carefully before embarking on a relationship with a colleague. Be guided by common sense and consider potential conflicts of interest; it's also worth checking whether your employer has a policy on such matters.

However professional you are, others might be quick to assume that your judgement is clouded. A relationship between senior manager and junior staff member is particularly problematic, and may require one of you to consider a change of company or role.

If it's early days and you're not sure whether your romance has staying power, be as discreet as possible and keep it between yourselves. If you become an established couple, it is worth considering letting people know, with a view to pre-empting any gossip.

Never flaunt your romance in front of colleagues: displays of intimacy will undermine your professional-ism and make others uncomfortable. You will gain the respect of others by showing restraint.

Handled carefully, romance can thrive at work. However, if you find that mixing business with pleasure is affecting your work or your relationship adversely, assess your priorities and act decisively.

## OLD PEOPLE, RESPECT FOR

*'In the end, it's not the years in your life that count.
It's the life in your years.'*
ABRAHAM LINCOLN

Our perception of what constitutes 'elderly' is changing. Older people are staying healthier for longer and pride themselves on retaining their youth, so the business of respecting our elders can be tricky. In times past, the elderly occupied an elevated position in society and were treated deferentially, but this can now seem unnecessary or even patronising.

Some older people will still expect particularly considerate treatment, however, so exercise judgement. When travelling on public transport, offer your seat to a person who appears to need it more than you, but don't be offended if he or she declines or let this put you off making the same gesture in the future.

If you are in conversation with someone who is hard of hearing, avoid shouting or speaking more slowly than usual. Speak audibly and articulately, and be guided by them. Above all, be patient: older people are likely to take life more slowly than their younger companions.

If you are an older person, show reciprocal patience and respect for younger generations. A polite response will go a long way. Reacting in a prickly way to what you interpret as an over-the-top demonstration of respect will embarrass and discourage younger people from acting considerately in the future.

## ONLINE MANNERS

The online universe is about communication: people meet each other, share information, argue and discuss. Just because you are apparently interacting with a machine does not mean that manners should be forgotten.

Make it a general rule not to say anything online that you wouldn't be able to articulate face-to-face. The internet is supposed to facilitate communication, not to preside over its breakdown.

Don't use technology as a shield, masking your true feelings and personality. Be polite in emails, and never send or post messages that contain inflammatory language or sentiments that you wouldn't normally express.

Don't be a troll, skulking behind the computer screen and dishing out negativity, or more seriously, threatening people you can't see. On the other hand, avoid becoming an online bore: posts or blogs that enumerate the minutiae of your day in tedious detail may hold a horrible fascination for others, but won't make you popular.

Finally, remember that the internet should enhance your life, not become a substitute for it.

*See also Social Networking, Trolls*

## OSTENTATION

'Ostentatious' is no longer a pejorative word – flash cars, dazzling jewellery and gourmet meals are casually shown off to whoever will pay attention. There are whole industries of publicists, agents, managers and spokespeople who have turned showing off into a profession; rafts of the media who report upon it; and whole sections of society who enjoy nothing more than reading about it.

We've come a long way from the unassuming 'less is

more' discretion of the past, but we still admire the
restraint of those who remain more private than public,
more whispered-about than talking-about.

But don't go too far. Not flaunting riches and success
is one thing, being ostentatiously shabby and low-key
when everyone knows you're worth millions is just
irritating for those of us who'd love to prove how much
fun we'd have with the money.

*See also Understatement*


## OVERFAMILIARITY

The chill dread that accompanies the overfamiliar
person can be triggered by the subtlest of clues: a
gratuitous touch of your hand, a conspiratorial wink in
conversation, an insistence on calling you 'darling' when
you are still struggling to remember their name.

A similar horrified fascination dawns when you meet
someone at a dinner party who within seconds is
confessing their inability to hold on to a boyfriend.

Taking intimacy for granted is a sure-fire way to
estrange; slapping your new boss on the back on your
first day will alienate rather than ingratiate.

If familiarity breeds contempt, overfamiliarity
propagates pity and dread. While it can be endearing at
first, overfamiliarity often masks insecurities or worse,
idleness and lack of genuine interest. People who think

that they can go straight to Intimacy without passing Go
need to put in more groundwork to earn your friendship.
*See also Friendship*

## OVERREACTION

It is no longer enough to win a competition with a smile
and a discreet fist pump. We must scream and clutch our
faces in disbelief.

Tutting and shaking our heads at a supermarket
queue-barger no longer holds enough weight; we feel
compelled to rage about the offence on social media.
Patting a child on the head is no longer sufficient; they
must be congratulated at every turn, praised effusively
for merely trying. We live in an age of burgeoning
overreaction and it's getting exhausting.

Where do we go, then, when reacting to real
achievement, real despair, real anger? Strangely, back
round the circle to the smallest reaction of all: silence.
The respectful silence that greets a funeral cortège is
often far more affecting than audible wailing.

Similarly, you know you have fed a roomful of people
well when they're too busy eating to remember to
compliment the chef or photograph their food.

Overreaction is often justifiable, however, when it's a
form of feigned politeness that masks unworthy feelings.
This is the case with the pleased, knowing smile of the

passed-over award nominee or the 'Wow! Isn't it gorgeous!' when your child proudly hands you a misshapen clay egg cup on your birthday.

## OVERSHARING

We are all in danger of becoming habitual oversharers, spurred on by the examples and encouragement of our peers online. But those 'liking' your post about your stress-related skin condition may be doing so less out of genuine sympathy and more from a position of fascination.

On the other hand, sharing personal experiences can be a brave and selfless way of raising awareness about an issue, whether it's a medical complaint, a bereavement, or a political or social problem.

Before you share personal information about yourself on a public platform, ask yourself what you're hoping to achieve. If your motives are altruistic — awareness-raising or fundraising for a charity, for example — go ahead. If you're merely looking for validation and approval, keep that personal information to yourself.

Never overshare on behalf of others: publicly 'outing' somebody, in any form, is unacceptable.

## OYSTERS

Oysters are served in their shell. They should come already shucked (i.e. detached), but use your fork to prise the flesh from the shell if any sticks. Squeeze lemon juice over them, then pick up the shell, bring it to your lips and tilt it to slide the oyster into your mouth. If you prefer, spear the oyster with a fork. Don't chew it; swallow it whole.

Oysters are believed to have aphrodisiac qualities, so beware the implications of ordering a dozen on a first date.

PARTIES TO
PUNCTUATION

## PARTIES

*'I don't know a lot about politics, but I can recognise
a good party man when I see one.'*
MAE WEST

No two gatherings are ever the same, and even with an
identical venue, refreshment and music, no party can
ever be replicated.

Atmosphere is an elusive commodity, and it falls to
the host to create the right conditions and make your
guests comfortable. This means ensuring that they have
plenty to eat and drink, and that everyone is socialising.
Introduce your friends to each other, and ensure that no
one is left out. Don't take this too far, however;
interrupting animated conversations and dragging
people across the room because there is 'someone they
must meet' is very bad manners.

If there are spills or breakages, clear up quickly and
efficiently, and don't make a fuss. As a host, it is your
duty to stay to the bitter end – even if a party is evidently
flagging, you should not leave your guests simply to
'get on with it'.

If you are a guest, respond to an invitation punctually
and make sure you actually show up if you accept. If
possible, allow yourself half an hour more than you think
you need to get ready; you will create the right impression and arrive in a better frame of mind.

Arrive in good time but avoid being early; your host

may be thrown into a panic by having to entertain whilst making last-minute preparations.

However stressful your day has been, leave your bad mood at the door. You are here to enjoy yourself and to help others do the same.

A drink will help you unwind, but be careful not to overdo it. This also applies to food; avoid stationing yourself by the buffet all evening, and never pursue a tray of canapés through a crowded room.

When engaged in one-on-one conversation, give the other person your full attention and be as lively and stimulating as you can. Never look over his or her shoulder for an escape route or a better offer. It is worth having one or two techniques up your sleeve to detach yourself from a conversation that is going nowhere.

When you leave, always thank your host warmly and follow up with a note of thanks.

*See also Buffets; Canapés; Conversation; Hosting*


### PAUSES

Don't be fooled into thinking that, in conversational terms, silence is simply a point when no one is talking. A pause in conversation can speak volumes, and should be used consciously and discerningly. If someone asks you what you think of their new fringe and you pause before blandly answering, 'It really suits you', your hesitation might be interpreted as doubt or insincerity, rather than honest reflection.

Pauses can also be used for positive effect, to create drama and tension in your discourse or when delivering a speech: your audience is transfixed as they wait for your next utterance, and expectations are high.

If you follow this suspense-laden pause with a humorous remark you will be applauded for your comic timing.

## PERFUME

Exercise moderation when it comes to perfume; don't overpower those around you. Be particularly aware of overuse in confined spaces such as cars or aeroplanes – your love of lavender or tuberose may cause those in the immediate vicinity to suffer sudden sneezing fits. Wear a delicate fragrance for daytime and save stronger scents for the evening.

## PERSONAL SPACE

If somebody is standing too close to you, you may start to feel troubled and as though you want to step backwards. You might be focusing less on what the other person is saying, and more on how close they are to you.

Perceptions of what constitutes an invasion of personal space are often dictated by culture. Some

cultures will prefer to communicate at a respectful distance, while others will be more comfortable with a close-quarters exchange, possibly involving physical gestures such as a hand on the arm or shoulder.

The latter approach can be trickier to handle in a work context, but you can establish some boundaries by suggesting that conversations take place seated at a meeting table or with a desk between you.

In a social environment or at a networking event, you can try to increase your personal space by introducing another person to your conversation, or by turning outwards to gesture at something or comment on your surroundings.

If someone attempts to give you an unwanted hug or kiss, promptly extending a hand for a handshake instead will help to establish the same boundaries.

On a non-physical plane, unwanted breaches of our solitude can also feel like invasions of our personal space. As we become increasingly insulated from the outside world by technology, real-world attempts by other people to smile, make eye contact or start a conversation can make us feel like our privacy has been compromised.

While it's important to preserve your personal space, this shouldn't be at the expense of any intimacy at all. So get out there and start interacting with people — just don't stand too close.

*See also Lifts*

## PETS

If you are an animal-owner, you are likely to be an animal-lover, happy to share a bed with your cat, thrilled by the twittering of your budgerigar, and undeterred by your dog's slobbering. Remember that not everybody shares your enthusiasm.

Check first, and if your visitors are hesitant or confess to an allergy to cat hair, don't inflict your animals upon them. Exclaiming 'she really likes you' as your visitor flinches from the clawing of your cat simply won't do.

If you have guests, keep pets out of their bedrooms, unless enthusiastically requested to do otherwise. Don't anthropomorphise your pets in public: you may think of them as furry near-humans, but cloying 'conversations', complete with baby voices and endearments, will embarrass your visitors.

*See also Dogs*

## PHOTOGRAPHS

We all have an instinct to record happy occasions, but make sure that your insistence on a photo opportunity isn't preventing others from enjoying the moment. Make sure you're not interrupting meaningful conversations, and avoid using a blinding flash or taking endless variations of the same shot.

Ask permission from somebody before you take their photograph and exercise caution before sharing a picture

of somebody else online. If there's any danger that it will cause embarrassment, resist the urge. Never post photographs of other people's children on social media.

If you're invited to look at a photograph on someone else's phone, be wary of scrolling through the rest of the album: you never know what you might inadvertently stumble upon.

*See also Food, Photographing; Selfies*


## POCKET SQUARES

Adding an extra sartorial dimension to a suit or blazer, a pocket square is primarily decorative; if you have to use it as a handkerchief, put it away in your trouser pocket afterwards.

A pocket square need not be square – it can poke out in a triangular point, be pulled into a puff, or be folded into a more elaborate style. However you choose to wear it, your pocket square shouldn't match your tie.

*See also Handkerchiefs*


## POLITENESS

Politeness is not a failsafe measure of manners: you can be punctilious about opening doors, pulling out chairs and walking on the kerbside edge of pavements – but still be appallingly rude.

Real manners are practised by people who know how to make others around them feel at ease, how to make the world feel a more civilised, friendly and calm place, and who like to put others' comfort ahead of their own.

If your own idea of politeness means you've created a formal seating plan for your dinner party, good manners demand that when your guests sit themselves down at random, you just smilingly go with the flow.

If insisting on opening a door for someone means that you have to shove your way past them in the first place, then why not stand back, relax and acknowledge their own kindness in holding the door open for you?

Politeness may sometimes seem old-fashioned and impractical, but it shouldn't be abandoned entirely — it is part of the social contract we all tacitly enter into to make the world more harmonious.

We need to preserve politeness as an ingredient in the cocktail of manners that makes our world a better place, somewhere where basic survival is transformed into a more subtle pleasure.

## POLITICS, DISCUSSING

The world would be a bland place if no one ever argued about politics. However, emotions frequently run high around political issues, and you should therefore treat this issue with care and respect.

If you're in an environment where a stand-up, passionate political row is not desirable (an office or dinner party where you're being introduced to your fiancé(e)'s parents etc.), then it is probably a good idea to avoid the topic of politics altogether, or at least gauge the prevailing political climate. In these circumstances, a heartfelt consensus is bonding, whereas dissent is likely to be damaging.

In a less sensitive environment, there is no reason not to join the fray. Just be sure that you know what you're talking about and have the facts straight before you lay into anyone. Your arguments will be more persuasive if you keep calm, listen to other people and treat their views with respect.

*See also Arguments; Brexit*


## PORT

Port is traditionally served after pudding with the coffee or cheese course. If you are at an informal dinner party or a restaurant, no ritual will be involved, but take more care at a formal dinner, in which case you should not take a sip before the Loyal Toast (toast to the Queen) is proposed by the host.

A port decanter will be placed on the table so that you can help yourself and then pass it on. Always pass the port to the left. If the port passes you by without your glass being filled, don't ask for the port and make it change direction. Just send your empty glass after the port decanter and ask for it to be filled.

*See also Digestifs; Formal Dinners*

## POSTCARDS

When picture-postcards were first sent in the 19th century, they were the Victorian equivalent of today's text message – pithy, informal and to the point.

Now sadly falling from favour, a snail-mail postcard still serves as a thoughtful gesture in the age of email and SMS, a reminder that you are thinking of a person.

There is little etiquette surrounding postcards: you do not normally have to start them with a salutation (you can go straight into the message), and you do not need to employ any particular sign-off.

If possible, avoid the obvious postcard clichés like 'wish you were here', and inject your note with personality – a humorous observation or a personal reference or reminiscence. Try to write, stamp and post it while you're still on your travels, rather than putting it off until you're back on home ground.

## POSTPONING

Postponing a meeting, date or other social event is unavoidable from time to time, but to postpone politely you must be prompt. Make contact with the other party as soon as you know that you're unable to make the appointed date. If you leave your postponement to the eleventh hour — unless you have a very good reason — you will show a lack of respect for the person you're meeting. Do not become a serial postponer; it is easy to acquire a reputation in such matters, and people will stop taking future arrangements seriously. In short, you will no longer receive any invitations to attend anything of interest.

Taking the time to ring reassures others that you value their time and intend to honour future commitments, but an email or text message is acceptable if you are unable to get through by phone. Choose your wording carefully to avoid appearing offhand.

Explain your reasons as honestly as possible. If a clash arises, you should usually honour the first commitment you made, but in exceptional circumstances, a friend will understand if you explain the pressing nature of the alternative. Try and reschedule your engagement as soon as possible.

*See also Cancelling; Flaking*

## PREGNANCY

In the early and late days of pregnancy it is easy to imagine that you deserve to have better manners shown to you than your fellow unpregnant woman or man.

Early on, you may be feeling tired and queasy; in the final weeks, you're sharing an already cramped body with a lodger who keeps you awake at night and has distorted your physique beyond all recognition. In both cases, you are surely entitled to better treatment from those around you.

Pregnant women should therefore be given a seat on the Tube, offered a hand with bags, and shown every possible consideration. If you are pregnant yourself, remember to react as if you are being shown beautiful manners, not as if it is your right and expectation.

The minefield of establishing whether someone is pregnant often means that extra-considerate treatment is withheld for fear of causing offence. Offer your seat on the train to a portly woman at your own risk: there's a chance you'll offend her as much as you wanted to look out for her. When someone says that they are not drinking, don't respond, 'Oh right, not in your condition,' unless you have a disregard for your own personal safety.

Pregnant women should be prepared to be assertive if necessary: wear that 'Baby on Board' badge even if it makes you cringe, tell someone that you'd appreciate their seat, or simply place your hand wearily into the small of your back in the international gesture for 'Yes, it's okay, I am pregnant'.

## PREENING

Whether it's a quick touch-up of lipstick in your rear-view mirror or a full makeover on the train to work, our grooming and preening habits are increasingly making the transition from behind the bathroom door into the public realm.

We all like to look our best, and a polished appearance can improve our performance and the impression we make on others. Don't undermine this positive impression by revealing the process behind it – keep brushing, blotting and touch-ups for the work loos or the back of a cab.

Don't let your vanity inconvenience others, either: if a friend suggests a photograph, avoid delaying the process by rushing off to take care of your shiny forehead. And while it's fine to check your mascara hasn't run while on public transport, painting your nails, tweezing your eyebrows or inspecting your spots will not make you popular with your fellow passengers.

## PRESENTS

A time-honoured way of showing affection or gratitude, or of marking rites of passage such as birth or marriage, the giving and receiving of presents is one of life's pleasures. Presents should always be given in good faith and with the intention of pleasing the recipient.

A thoughtful present should be appreciated

regardless of cost: the time you have taken to think about what the other person will like will be apparent in your choice. However, if you do not know your recipient well, certain presents have enduring appeal and will always be appreciated.

If possible, do some research to avoid making a basic error – the bottle of whisky to the teetotaller or the chocolates to the dieter. Remember that present-giving is not a competition, so there is no need to go over the top. A very extravagant present might embarrass the recipient and create a sense of reciprocal obligation.

When selecting presents for those close to you, think carefully about their tastes, hobbies and passions. Never fall into the trap of buying a present that you really want for yourself, and that you intend to use, borrow or adopt.

Remember what you have given in the past. A repeat present suggests that you take the whole business lightly – unless the recipient loved something so much the first time that they specifically asked for it again. Keep a list if your memory is poor. Try not to agonise over choice and never try to match the anticipated value of a reciprocal present. Giving and receiving are separate activities, and this is not the time to weigh up the *quid pro quo*.

To ensure that giving is truly better than being on the receiving end, take the time to plan. A last-minute trip to the shops will leave you frazzled and spoil the experience.

Check with the giver whether or not they are happy for

you to open the present there and then — if it is not yet your birthday, for example, they may prefer you to wait until the day itself.

Whatever the item, react with enthusiasm and thanks. Disappointment, distaste or just indifference must be hidden at all costs.

If appropriate, ask questions about the present or reflect on when you will use it. For all but the most casually given gifts, a written thank you is appropriate.
*See also Christenings; Engagement; Re-Gifting; Wedding Lists*

## PRONUNCIATION

If someone mispronounces a word, it is rude to correct their pronunciation — they will feel crushed and foolish. The exception is if someone mispronounces your name, in which case it is fine gently to repeat it with the correct pronunciation — perhaps with an acknowledgement if it happens to be unusual or difficult to get right.

The tactful option is to reintroduce the word that has been mispronounced into the conversation: by using the correct pronunciation you will be alerting them to the mistake. The other person can either choose to rectify their error in future, or stick doggedly to their own version.

While everyone admires linguistic ability, resist any desire to show off your skills by overpronouncing foreign words. Foreign words used in English conversation are usually gently anglicised; guttural or phlegmatic consonants, trilled 'rs' and exaggerated glottal stops are unnecessary.

## PROPOSAL, MARRIAGE
*'Grow old with me! The best is yet to be.'*
ROBERT BROWNING

A proposal of marriage requires planning. If all goes well and you become engaged, friends and family will want you to recall the story of the proposal again and again, so even if you opt for a low-key evening at home with a bottle of champagne hidden in the fridge, ensure the occasion is memorable and carefully thought through.

It is traditional for whoever is doing the proposing to have an engagement ring ready, but traditions are less carefully followed in an age when women propose to men, men to men, and women to women.

Some couples prefer to choose the ring or rings together; in that case, an alternative meaningful token might be given instead.

It's not compulsory for the proposer to get on one knee, but it can make the occasion more memorable and ceremonial. The proposer must sound confident and clear when he or she pops the question – the other person doesn't want to be guessing whether or not they have heard correctly.

If the answer is 'yes', celebrations will inevitably

follow. If it's 'no', the refuser should offer to give the ring or other item back — it's up to the other person as to whether to accept its return.

Equally, if the recipient doesn't like the ring that's been chosen, he or she should gently and tactfully tell the proposer in good time.

*See also Engagement*


## PROSECCO

Virtually unheard of in Britain just a decade ago, sparkling wine from the Veneto region of Italy is now so popular that it has spawned dedicated prosecco bars, vans and evenings (also known as Fizz Fridays).

With a more palatable reputation than cava and packing a smaller punch to the wallet than champagne, prosecco is not solely drunk in celebration: it can be ordered by the glass in bars and pubs and brought along to parties, picnics and dinners.

There are three levels of prosecco fizziness: the most effervescent *spumante*, the gently bubbling *frizzante*, and the entirely flat *tranquillo*. It is usually served in champagne flutes, and bottles should be opened in the same way as champagne bottles.

*See also Champagne*

## PS AND QS

Opinions differ as to the origin of the phrase 'ps and qs'. Some say that it was once shouted in pubs when things were getting a little rowdy – 'Mind your Pints and Quarts!' – these being the main measurements of drinks before the Second World War.

Others say that it was an old printers' saying, a reminder to typesetters to pay attention to the details.

Regardless of its origins, it has been common in post-Victorian Britain as shorthand for 'to mind your manners' or, more specifically, to say both 'please' (ps) and 'thank you' (thank-qs).

This is inevitably a child's first introduction to manners, and parents are haunted by the repetition of 'Say please/ thank-you!' every few minutes for the first five, ten or fifteen years of their child's existence.

In this case, the tedium of repetition is surely justified – a child who doesn't mind their ps and qs, the most basic of good manners, is being given a poor start in life.

## PUBLIC TRANSPORT

Basic courtesies are easily forgotten on public transport, particularly when delays and overcrowding cause even the most unflappable of us to become frustrated.

Don't let your irritation affect your manners, and remember to offer your seat to those who need it more than you do. If you're concerned that someone might be offended by the assumption that they are elderly, pregnant or infirm, it is best to vacate your seat anyway, move away and hope that your intended recipient will gravitate towards it.

Proximity heightens tension and amplifies your behaviour, so be considerate if using a mobile phone, eating, drinking, listening to music or carrying lots of bulky luggage.

If a fellow passenger is causing a minor annoyance, it's usually best to ignore it. If they are being particularly rude or intimidating to you or another person, confront them as long as it feels safe to do so — others may feel emboldened to join in and offer strength in numbers.

Smile and thank others who act in a patient or considerate way, including the driver and any staff.

*See also Headphones; Preening; Quiet Zones; Trains*

## PUBS

Observe and respect the atmosphere of a pub. If other drinkers are sitting alone or quietly chatting in small groups, don't ruin the mood with loud conversations or raucous games of pool.

Likewise, if you are in a busy town centre pub after work on a Friday there's no point complaining about the rowdy group of office workers at the table next to you. Pubs are very sociable places, so be prepared to exchange small talk with strangers – especially if a big sporting event is being shown.

If a group of you are drinking together it is usual for people to take it in turns to buy a round. Don't opt out of rounds, or hang back; you shouldn't have to be reminded that it's your turn.

Tipping is not usually necessary in a pub, but if you're a regular customer or feel you've received particularly notable service you may like to offer the bar staff a drink. *See also Bars*

## PUNCTUALITY

*'I have always been a quarter of an hour before my time, and it has made a man of me.'*
LORD NELSON

Repeatedly failing to be punctual is bad manners because it discounts the value of other people's time. By being late you are effectively forcing the people you are meeting to waste their time. Hanging around waiting for someone is deeply frustrating.

By being late, you will always arrive at your meeting at a disadvantage – flustered and apologetic. Conversely, being punctual always scores bonus points. You will come across as someone who cares about other people, and is efficient, organised and reliable.

Between the vagaries of public transport, meetings that overrun, and random home emergencies, you can't

expect to be unfailingly punctual, but in this day and age there is no excuse for not warning someone that you're running late.

Ideally, call the person you're meeting to tell them, with profuse apologies, that you are delayed. If the situation looks out of control (total rail shutdown, terrorist alert or a sick child), let them know as soon as possible and reschedule.

## PUNCTUATION

Punctuation isn't voluntary. Full stops, commas and colons are the only things that stand between cogent prose and chaotic streams-of-consciousness. Don't be fooled by the language of modern messaging into thinking that punctuation is optional.

If you're not confident in your ability to punctuate, use grammar-checking software, look up queries online, or ask a trusted friend or colleague to read important documents or correspondence for you.

A misuse or absence of punctuation can render your writing open to misinterpretation. Punctuation is frequently dismissed as the preserve of the pedantic and old-fashioned, but when used correctly, it clarifies rather than confuses.

*See also Email; Grammar*

QUEEN, HM THE
TO QUITTING

## QUEEN, HM THE

A formal encounter with The Queen will be carefully organised and choreographed, so you should wait to be presented rather than initiate an introduction. Men should bow from the head only, and women should make a small curtsey. Neither movement should be prolonged or exaggerated. It is acceptable but less usual to shake hands.

Address The Queen as 'Your Majesty' and subsequently as 'Ma'am' (to rhyme with 'jam'). As far as conversation is concerned, you may be briefed in advance as to how much time is available. However, allow yourself to be guided during the audience itself. Relax and behave as naturally as possible.

If you are introducing another person to The Queen, simply state the name of the person as follows:

'May I present John Smith, Your Majesty?'

When conversing with The Queen, substitute 'Your Majesty' for 'you'.

When writing to The Queen, letters should be addressed to her private secretary unless they are from those who are personally known to her. Address your letter 'Madam' or 'May it please Your Majesty' and close with 'I have the honour to remain, Madam, Your Majesty's humble and obedient servant'. In the body of the letter, substitute 'Your Majesty' for 'you' and 'Your Majesty's' for 'your'.

*See Debrett's Handbook for more information.*

*See also Bowing; Ma'am; Royal Family*

QUEUING

*'An Englishman, even if he is alone, forms an orderly queue of one.'*
GEORGE MIKES

Where other nationalities congregate, the British queue. Whether you're catching a bus, buying a ticket or doing your weekly shop, you will join an orderly line of people.

The compulsion to queue dates back to the days of rationing during and after the World Wars of the last century, when queuing effectively meant the difference between an empty plate and a plate filled with the delights of powdered egg and dense bread.

Communal complaining in a queue remains a rare pleasure: there is a liberating anonymity in speaking to someone whose back is to you. The person in front will usually turn enough so that you can hear them but not enough so that you exchange eye contact and graduate to personal interaction and the suggestion of intimacy that this might entail.

For visitors to the UK, the art of queuing must seem eccentric at best and infuriating at worst, but queue-barging is a serious offence and will usually result in the culprit being sent unceremoniously to the end of the line.

Queuing does require participation, however, and anyone who isn't fully committed to moving forward an inch for every inch that opens up will earn almost as

much disapproval of the crowd queuing behind as the shameless barger.

If you're with family or a group of friends, nominate one person to join a queue if possible, rather than clogging it up with unnecessary people and luggage.

When more than one queue is operating in tandem (at airport check-in desks, for example), nothing can quite match the joy of being in the one that beats its rivals. Such moments of pure adrenalin are what life is all about.

## QUIET ZONES

A designated quiet zone is precisely what it says. Don't subject your fellow passengers to mobile phone conversations, music leaking through headphones, or loud chats with friends.

If someone else is being noisy or disruptive, politely ask them to keep it down, perhaps prefacing your remark with 'I'm not sure if you're aware, but this is a quiet zone.' If they persist, inform a member of staff, and wait for them to be removed.

*See also Mobile Phones; Public Transport; Trains*

## QUINOA

It's pronounced *keen-wah.*

## QUITTING

Handing in your resignation is something you can't go back on, so it's worth getting it right. Manage the process as carefully as you would handle any other business endeavour; no matter how fed up you are, you will regret burning bridges.

The compulsion to quit spectacularly, sweeping into your boss's office and telling them exactly what you think of them, is sometimes strong, but the exhilaration will soon turn to remorse when you find you can't get a reference.

Even if you hate your boss, be polite and positive when you quit: think of your soon-to-be former colleagues as part of your network of the future.

When you speak to your boss to hand in your resignation, be professional and make sure you've checked your contract for your notice period or other terms that might apply.

Emphasise the positive about your time at the company but add that it's time to move on and that you've found an opportunity that 'fits you better'. You don't need to say too much, but offer to help during the transition, preparing handover notes, recruiting or training up your replacement.

Whatever the job, accompany any spoken intent with a formal letter of resignation stating when your last day will be; it looks more professional and will clear up any uncertainties about notice periods.

Making a clean break is a useful and transferrable skill — it can be applied not just to jobs, but to relationships, voluntary roles and contracts, whether with your mobile phone company, your broadband provider or your gym.

RECYCLING
TO RSVPS

## RECYCLING

With alarming studies on our environment published every week, the pressure to recycle has never been greater.

Even if you are sceptical about threats of global warming, recycling household items is so straightforward that there is no reason to avoid it: assign a separate bin or box for recyclable materials and the council will usually take care of the rest.

If you don't find the scientific evidence sufficiently compelling, consider the social motivation. Acting blasé about environmental concerns can make you appear selfish and narrow-minded. An impressive array of recycling boxes, on the other hand, will be applauded.

There's also the economic incentive to consider: remembering to bring your 'bag for life' to the supermarket allows you to dodge the carrier bag charge, while many coffee chains offer discounts if you bring your own non-disposable cup.

*See also Environment, Respecting*


## REFUSING

*'The only man who is really free is the one who can turn down an invitation to dinner without giving any excuse.'*
JULES RENARD

Refusing graciously, without causing offence, is a vital social skill. Whatever the occasion, you have the right to turn an invitation down, but whether you have a legitimate

reason for doing so or are simply indifferent to the offer, good manners demand that you provide an excuse.

Simply saying 'No, thank you' seems blunt and could offend; indicating that you have, for example, another commitment softens the blow. Do not, however, make the mistake of dressing your refusal with elaborate excuses. Less is more, and over-embroidering will arouse suspicion.

There will be occasions when you are confronted with an inability to read social signals, and at that point, your good manners may have to be compromised. If you really don't want to comply (a persistent suitor, for example) a point-blank refusal will get the message across.

## RE-GIFTING

Whether it's a bottle of wine, a box of chocolates or a pair of cufflinks, re-gifting is the art of passing on a present that was originally given to you by someone else.

In a world of waste and excess, there is a legitimate argument for recycling in this way. How much better to give that sequinned sweater to a flamboyant friend than to leave it languishing unworn at the back of your wardrobe?

The theory has logic, but the practice has to be watertight. No one must ever know: not the original giver nor the next-in-line receiver. Ensure that the receiver is at least six degrees separated from the giver, and that the 're-gift' is shop-fresh and unmarked.

Check the present has not been personalised in any way by the original giver — it's hard to recover if your recipient discovers your initials monogrammed in the corner of that silk scarf you've just given them.

Finally, be careful not to boast — never tell anyone about your talent for re-gifting. They'll never give you anything and will be forever suspicious about their own presents from you. And don't present the re-gift with too much flourish, just in case. Recycling and economising are all very well, but deep down, you know that what you are doing is ... cheap.

*See also Presents*

## RELIGION

*'There are no atheists on a turbulent aircraft.'*
ERICA JONG

Religion affects everyone, and if you live in a city or town, it's likely that you will see different religions observed on a daily basis, whether in dress, attitude or behaviour.

There are, obviously, codes of behaviour particular to each religion. The best approach is to tread carefully, respect differences and adjust your own behaviour to suit the environment in which you find yourself. If travelling in a Muslim country, for example, respect dress codes and physical protocols: men and women do not usually shake hands; rather the man will place his hand on his heart and bow his head slightly.

Always treat priests, monks, imams and rabbis with politeness and respect. Dietary restrictions should be taken seriously and accommodated.

When it comes to your social life, it can be harder to observe these sensitivities, but whatever your beliefs, cynicism can easily start to look rude. So don't be too quick to judge the Jehovah's Witness, the Hare Krishna monk, the born-again Christian. You might actually learn something from listening for five minutes.

## RESTAURANTS

'Dining out' describes a range of eating experiences, but restaurant rules are universal. As the customer, a little charm goes a long way.

Treating your waiter or waitress respectfully will enhance your experience, but attempting to befriend them is inappropriate. Allow serving staff to do their jobs discreetly.

Whenever possible, make a reservation, and particularly if you are dining in a group. Notify the restaurant of any special dietary or access requirements in advance.

If you are unhappy with the table you are allocated, ask politely if you can move, but do this before you sit down to minimise disturbance.

If you are hosting a gathering, it is perfectly acceptable (and may save time and fuss) to take control of the wine list, but defer to anyone who demonstrates an intimate

knowledge of the cellar. On a date, share the
responsibility and make the selection a talking point.

Many restaurants now offer tap, as well as bottled,
water. There is no shame in requesting it. When dining
in a group, try to agree on the number of courses. Once
you have chosen, close your menu so that the waiter or
waitress knows he or she can take your order.

If you know that someone else will be picking up the
bill, choose modestly. If you are footing the bill, suggest
to your guests that they have free rein.

Normally, everyone at the table is served at the same
time. Wait until all dishes have arrived at the table before
starting. If yours is lagging behind, insist the others
start, and wait a few minutes before quietly enquiring as
to where yours is.

If you are unhappy with your food, let the waiter or
waitress know discreetly and with minimal fuss, and request
any necessary (and reasonable) changes. Keep things
pleasant, and don't blame the person who served you.
Angry complaints may spoil your companions' evening.

If you have organised the event, it is your
responsibility to pay (unless another arrangement has
been agreed beforehand). If you are splitting the bill
amongst a group, divide it equally unless certain people
have very obviously consumed less food or wine than the
rest of the table. Niggling about the comparative cost of
dishes and drinks will look stingy.

A service charge is often added to the bill

automatically, but if not, always leave an appropriate tip unless service has been terrible. Leaving a tip in cash might make it more likely to go to the service staff instead of the management.

*See also Bill, Paying the; Complaining; Tipping*


## ROAD RAGE

*'Anybody going slower than you is an idiot and anybody going faster than you is a maniac'.*
GEORGE CARLIN

Despite technology promising to make our journeys more comfortable and convenient than ever, road rage is at an all-time high.

But giving in to frustration when you're stuck behind a muck-spreader doing 20 miles an hour on a narrow country road won't get you to your destination any quicker. Blind fury can impede our judgment, prompting rash or dangerous actions.

So instead of overtaking impulsively on a blind corner, try to remain calm by playing music or listening to a podcast or audiobook. If possible, make a hands-free call to let relevant parties know that you're running late (or ask a passenger to do so).

If you have incurred another driver's fury, either don't react at all and pretend that honk was meant for someone else, or smile and mouth, 'Sorry!'

Road rage is now being joined by air rage, pavement rage, carpark rage, train rage and even school drop-off rage. In our increasingly angry world, 'drive carefully' is now an adage for all walks of life.
*See also Anger; Driving; Zebra Crossings*


## ROYAL ASCOT

The dress code for racegoers is clearly prescribed and will vary depending on the area of the course you will be frequenting.

If you're visiting the Windsor Enclosure, smart attire is encouraged but no formal dress code applies. Fancy dress, novelty and branded clothing or replica sportswear are not permitted.

In the Queen Anne and Village Enclosures, women must wear a hat, headpiece or fascinator, and tops should not be strapless and must cover the midriff. Men must wear a suit and tie.

In the Royal Enclosure, women must wear a hat with a substantial headpiece, and shoulders and midriff should not be on display. Dresses or skirts should be of 'modest' length, defined as falling just above the knee or longer.

Men must wear black or grey morning dress with a waistcoat. A top hat must be worn throughout the Royal Enclosure, except in a private box.
*See also Hats, Morning Dress*

## ROYAL FAMILY

There is no accepted code of behaviour for encounters with royalty, but adhering to the traditional forms of address will help ease anxiety.

When meeting any member of the Royal Family, men should bow from the neck, and women should make a small curtsey. A handshake is also acceptable.

For male members of the Royal Family, use 'Your Royal Highness' and subsequently 'Sir'. A female member of the Royal Family should be addressed as 'Your Royal Highness' followed by 'Ma'am' (to rhyme with 'jam'). The exception is The Queen, who is addressed as 'Your Majesty' followed by 'Ma'am'.

Should you happen upon a member of the Royal Family during their time off, allow them the freedom to go about their business as an ordinary person. Assume that to royalty, being left alone is far from a discourtesy; it is a luxury.

*See also Bowing; Queen, HM The*


## RSVPS

Reply to invitations promptly and using the appropriate medium. If you received an invitation by post it is appropriate to send a handwritten reply; if someone has invited you by email you can reciprocate; if a phone number is given, it is acceptable to call.

If you have been invited to a big event, such as a wedding, a reply card is often included – if that's the case, use this to respond. If you'd like to add anything, such as an explanation as to why you can't attend the event, this should be done in a separate letter.

A reply to official functions and formal private invitations (including weddings) should be sent, if possible, on headed writing paper and written in the third person. State the name of any guests you are bringing if the invitation has been addressed to you 'and Partner' or 'and Guest.' Reiterate the date and time in the body of the letter.

*See also Invitations; Debrett's Handbook*

SATNAV TO
SWEARING

## SATNAV

In-car navigation systems have prevented many a long
and scenic detour, but they are not infallible: listen to
that inner voice of doubt before you gamely follow your
SatNav's instruction to turn off an A-road onto a
narrow dirt track.

Programme your SatNav with your destination
address before you set off so that you don't have to fiddle
with it while you're driving. If your spouse, partner or
other passenger queries its instructions, at least take
their opinion into account rather than brusquely
deferring to technology.

As a pedestrian using maps on your phone to get to
your destination, don't forget to glance up occasionally
to avoid colliding with other people

## SEAT, OFFERING ONE'S

In the past it was always considered courteous for a man
to offer his seat to a woman. It is now a more tricky
matter of personal judgement. There is no need to jump
up on the train or underground every time you see a
woman standing (unless she is pregnant or elderly, when
it is a definite requirement). But if circumstances are
particularly taxing or uncomfortable, and you're feeling
chivalrous, you should offer – she can always refuse.

## SEATING PLAN

A seating plan is a good way of organising your guests,
but can look over-formal and seem intimidating.

If you're hoping to create a relaxed atmosphere, don't
plan the seating arrangements; just make sure that
couples are separated and – if possible – genders
alternate. Sit those with similar interests together and
balance chatty people by sitting them at opposite ends of
the table. The host should sit near the door/kitchen.

Keep a close eye on proceedings during the first couple
of courses and pay attention to guests who are shy or have
come alone. If anyone is looking bored, you could suggest
that guests move around for pudding and coffee.

For official functions, a seating plan is important.
The principal guest is placed on the host's right.
Traditionally the principal guest's wife would be placed
on the host's left, the host's wife being placed on the
right of the principal guest. For large gatherings, such as
weddings, display a seating plan with numbered tables
and a list of guests at each table.

## SECRETS

*'Three may keep a secret if two of them are dead.'*
BENJAMIN FRANKLIN

There are two kinds of secrets: confidences that are made
to you in the course of normal conversations, and fully
acknowledged secrets.

Confidences are given to you freely and not on condition of secrecy, so you need to apply discretion in passing them on. However tempting it may be, do so only after examining your motives: are you trying to ingratiate yourself with another person, or to liven up a dull conversation?

If you make a conscious decision to share the confidence, make absolutely sure that this decision will not rebound on you: you will not want to be traced as the source of the 'leak'.

On the other hand, if you are sworn to secrecy, you are entering into a pact not to share the information entrusted to you. If you have any sense of honour or integrity, you will keep the secret at all costs, but if you know that you are incapable of doing so, warn the secret-sharer in advance.

*See also Whispering*

## SELF-CHECKOUT

You might relish the opportunity to avoid interpersonal contact, but self-checkouts are a ruse to save on staff salaries and make customers do the work. They are rarely more convenient or quicker than using a till overseen by a human.

If you do persist in using the self-checkout and the technology goes awry, make sure that you haven't inadvertently made a mistake – placing your item in the wrong area, scanning something twice or forgetting to weigh your bag – before furiously summoning the assistant. Human beings are even more susceptible to error than machines.

## SELF-RIGHTEOUSNESS

We live in a world of moral absolutes – the clean eater, the perfect parent, the ultra-marathon runner – all of whom lay claim to the moral high ground. For those of us stuck in the middle, it can be hard to hear anything other than the chorus of the righteous.

There are many ways to be self-righteous – about diet, about drinking or smoking, about composting or carbon footprints.

But why, when it's hard to find fault with its cause, is self-righteousness so unattractive – and usually so ineffective?

Real conviction tends to have a softer, more persuasive voice than the shrill cry of righteousness. If you're tempted to be self-righteous, ask yourself whether sanctimony ever charmed anyone into changing their mind.

More often, it will drive its targets into contrary wilfulness. Few things are harder to put up with than the annoyance of being set a good example; your ex-smoker friend pointedly waving away your smoke just makes you want to blow smoke rings in his face.

If you are intent on saving the world and everyone in it, remember that self-righteousness will get you nowhere – don't wear your cause on your sleeve but tucked firmly away in an inside pocket.

## SELFIES

The self-taken photograph – complete with artful lighting, side-on pose and subtle pout – is almost universal currency nowadays. Whether you're showing off your outfit or your 'squad', it's best to acknowledge the fact that you are, still, showing off, and accept all reactions – from admiration to ridicule – with equal good humour. If your social media feed is entirely devoted to selfies, it's a sure sign of self-absorption.

The selfie has largely replaced the autograph for celebrity encounters, too, but remember that it is considerably more invasive than merely proffering a programme to be signed. Approach your celebrity with caution – especially if he or she is out with family or a partner – and ask permission first to avoid capturing only the wide-eyed, startled grimace of someone afraid for their life.

*See also Photographs; Selfie Sticks*

## SELFIE STICKS

The selfie stick is one of the most divisive instruments of our age: for some, it's a symbol of the hollow narcissism that epitomises our modern society, and for others, a useful device for capturing a group photograph or notable landmark.

Selfie sticks are usually extendable, making them portable and unobtrusive when packed away, but take care that you're not impeding someone's path or view before whipping it out to full length. Note that some popular tourist sites have taken the step of banning selfie sticks. If that's the case, abide by the rules.

*See also Photographs; Selfies*


## SELFISHNESS

*'To love oneself is the beginning of a lifelong romance.'*
OSCAR WILDE

As you once again allow that pushy commuter to board the train ahead of you, forfeiting any hope of getting a seat, it can sometimes seem like the sharp-elbowed and selfish are inheriting the earth at the expense of the meek and unselfish.

Science has shown us that evolution is not about the survival of the species, but about the survival of the individual, the gene; an end which is inherently selfish. So to some extent – when we are fighting for the rights of our children to a decent education, or our parents to competent healthcare – we have to be selfish, and there is no point pretending otherwise.

We all have responsibilities as well as rights, however, and we should therefore aim to transcend our selfish genes little by little. It may be unrealistic to aim for a saintlike selflessness, but just try to add something unselfish to each day – one act of kindness, or one less selfish act.

## SHAMING, PUBLIC

We live in a time when anyone can wake up in the morning to find their name trending on Twitter.

First, somebody takes exception to something you say, do or wear. Then the offended party decides to record your crime and to share it with others. Soon it has gone viral, and before you know it a tabloid newspaper is calling your mother for a comment.

Sound terrifying? That's because it is.

The simplest solution, of course, is never to do or say anything offensive, either in public or on a public platform. If you're not sure what counts as offensive, don't do or say anything at all: shut down Facebook, cancel Twitter and delete Instagram, draw the curtains and sit silently on the sofa with a lifetime's supply of box sets.

If that's not an option, try to consider the consequences of any impulsive action, particularly one fuelled by fury or self-righteousness. However aggressive a cyclist is being, before you make a rude gesture through your window, remember we live in an age of helmet cams.

There is rarely any need to post an inflammatory comment on social media, so no matter how outraged you are by something you've read, close your browser, make a cup of tea and wait until you've calmed down.

Before you're tempted to shame somebody else, consider the effect it could have on their lives. OK, they've been rude, obnoxious or downright abusive, but what's to be gained by exposing their behaviour to the point of humiliation, social alienation or even a sacking?

## SHOPPING

Whether traipsing the high street or scouring the internet, our retail appetites are insatiable. While online shopping is quicker, more convenient and bypasses all social interaction, many still prefer the old-fashioned method.

Don't be intimidated by shops that treat you dismissively. You are the customer, and should be treated with respect — they will be the losers if their hostility discourages a potential sale.

Shop staff who talk amongst themselves as they serve you are simply being rude, and you are justified in complaining. On the other hand, you should never treat shop staff dismissively: don't take a call or use your phone while being served. If you are polite and engaging, you should find that you are rewarded with warm and generous service.

Shopping can and should be enjoyable. When it becomes unduly arduous, abort the mission unless it's essential. You will probably buy the wrong thing and irritate yourself and others in the process.
*See also Supermarkets*

## SHYNESS

Shyness is often felt most keenly by children, and can be strong enough to induce physical symptoms – blushing, stammering, even tears. Research has shown that this has more to do with as yet under-developed social skills, combined with unfamiliarity with a situation, than with a deeper form of introspection or social anxiety. While it seems like a character trait, it is more often just a symptom of the fear of the unknown.

In other words, ordinary shyness can be conquered by putting yourself into timidity-inducing scenarios and forcing yourself to join in; however daunting it feels the first time, the second time will be exponentially better.

Parents of naturally shy children are pivotal in influencing which way that shyness will go – gently introduced into non-threatening gatherings where they can develop their social skills at their own pace, these children will gradually shrug off their shyness.

When shyness accompanies you into adulthood, it can be isolating, and is easily mistaken for aloofness or an intolerance of other people's company. It can also be a

manifestation of acute self-consciousness, a painful hypersensitivity to the scrutiny of other people.

Shyness can be mitigated and even overcome by turning your attention away from yourself and focusing instead on the people around you. Remember that you are not the central component of every social interaction, but a small cog in the wheel. By protecting yourself behind a shield of good manners, you will find an antidote to your shyness.

## SILENCES

A discreet silence can serve a number of positive functions: signalling acquiescence, compliance or agreement. But not all silences are golden; they can also be a means of indicating disagreement, outrage or lack of cooperation. The context is critical.

Silences are powerful conversational tools, so use them with discretion. If you are silent, you may make the people around you uncomfortable. Some people find silence intolerable, and will feel the need to fill the vacuum — the silent treatment, aimed at a compulsive talker, is an act of aggression.

Never confuse small breaks in conversation with true silence: conversation is not invariably fluid, and short pauses are normal. Prolonged silences, on the other hand, are replete with meaning.

*See also Pauses*

'Smart casual' can be the hardest dress code to interpret, but the invitation and the type of event will give you some clue as to what to wear. A printed invitation suggests a smarter event than a text or email.

## 'Formal' Smart Casual for Men

For men, formal smart casual requires a jacket or blazer with trousers in cotton twill, linen, flannel or needlecord (not jeans), plus a shirt with a collar and smart shoes – not trainers or sandals. A sweater may be worn if it is cold. Ties are not necessary but carrying one is often a good tip, just in case.

Smart casual is usually a summer dress code, but if it is winter then opt for an overcoat rather than an anorak or parka. A tweed sports jacket may take the place of a blazer.

## 'Informal' Smart Casual for Men

Informal smart casual can usually be interpreted as neat, dark-coloured jeans for men. Other than in high summer or on the beach, trousers are better than shorts and polo shirts better than collarless t-shirts.

## 'Formal' Smart Casual for Women

For formal smart casual events, a smart day dress, worn with a jacket, is a safe choice for women. At more casual events, dress down a little – for example, smart trousers or a skirt, with a cardigan. Avoid wearing denim, unless it is immaculate and balanced with a tailored jacket and smart accessories. Also avoid high heels and wearing suits, as they look like business clothes. Sports clothes and sports shoes such as trainers are not suitable.

### 'Informal' Smart Casual for Women

Smart denim is usually acceptable, but sports or beach clothes should be avoided unless the occasion demands. However, too much tailoring and heels can also look wrong. If you are unsure, find out as much as possible about what other people are intending to wear. If that isn't possible, ask the host or hostess.

Be prepared to adjust your outfit at the last minute — for example swapping heels for flats, taking off dressy jewellery or removing a jacket and putting on a cardigan. *See also Lounge Suits; Underdressed*

### SMILING

Smile at strangers at your own risk: Brits, particularly urban-dwelling ones, are inherently suspicious of friendly overtures, however sincere they may be. You may be innocently full of the joys of life, but others are likely to interpret a broad smile as creepy, mocking, or worse, a come-on.

On the other hand, smiling in a social or business setting is an essential way of communicating warmth and establishing trust, even across language barriers. Keep your smile sincere and don't overdo it — a fixed, rictus grin can soon start to look lunatic.

Smiling when you answer the phone has a softening effect on your voice, which can put the other person immediately at ease.

Remember that smiles are infectious — and spreading a little infectious happiness can only be a good thing.

## SMOKING

If you are a smoker you may be feeling like a member of an endangered species, in more ways than one. Banned, excluded, disapproved of ... these days an attachment to nicotine has to be very strong indeed if you are going to withstand the social pariah status of the smoker.

Smoking is now banned in most public arenas, which has removed some of the responsibility from smokers, but even when out and about, dispose carefully of cigarette stubs and be mindful of anyone walking downstream of your exhalations.

Even in your own home, ask guests if they mind you smoking. In other people's homes, offer to go outside.

Non-smokers should also try to behave with some tolerance. If people around you are trying to smoke discreetly and considerately, it is rude to complain, bat away the smoke from your nose, mutter or cough ostentatiously. The efforts they are making to contain their addiction should be applauded, not derided.

SNEEZING

## SNEEZING

A largely unavoidable reflex, sneezing is at the acceptable
end of the bodily functions spectrum. Try to catch a
sneeze in a handkerchief and be as discreet as possible.
Additional sound effects for emphasis should be avoided.

If you feel a sneezing fit approaching, remove yourself
from company where possible.

## SNIFFING

Avoid sniffing in public by carrying tissues or a handkerchief in a pocket or bag.

Should you find yourself in the company of a sniffer,
avoid the temptation to offer them your handkerchief. If
you find it unbearable, remove yourself from earshot or
plug in some headphones.

*See also Nose Blowing*

## SNOBBISHNESS

*'The true definition of a snob is one who craves for what separates
men rather than for what unites them.'*
JOHN BUCHAN

A snob is someone who is blinded to the natural charms
of meeting someone new because they are so busy making
judgements about that person's accent, taste, how they
dress or where they went on holiday that year.

Handling a snob can be difficult: their aim is to

intimidate, which might make you defensive. Remember that often, the snobbier the person, the less socially secure they are. Armed with this insight, you can afford to be a little magnanimous and let them look down on you to their heart's content. If criticising the way you speak, or dress, or work, or eat is how the snobs get their kicks, then leave them to it, and revel in a sense of genuine social superiority.

## SOCIAL MEDIA

The semi-anonymous online world tempts us to behave in ways we would never contemplate in real life, so when you use social media, adopt the same approach that you would in face-to-face encounters.

Don't let social media replace all other methods of communication. There are times when letters and phone calls are still important, and it's better to send birthday cards than to leave a message via social media.

If you have important news to share – such as an engagement or the birth of a child – call those close to you rather than posting an announcement online.

Here are a few other 'netiquette' pointers to bear in mind:

- Check that your privacy settings prevent your posts from being seen by the public, and even then, never post anything that you wouldn't want a prospective employer to see.

- Refrain from posting cryptic or passive-aggressive comments such as 'On days like this, you find out who your real friends are.' You'll only make people feel paranoid that they've offended you.
- Never post negative comments on other people's photographs – the smiling-face-with-heart-eyes emoji is a universally acceptable response to pictures of anything from a poached egg to a newborn child.
- Ask permission before posting pictures of other people's children. Similarly, resist the temptation to overload your friends' feeds with adorable photographs of your own.
- Don't tag friends in embarrassing photographs – on a drunken night out, for example, or caught unawares in the middle of a burger.
- Don't use your personal account to promote your business or to publicise your political views. If necessary, set up a separate professional account.
- Don't let social media make you feel inadequate. A picture can be misleading – whether it's the filter that eliminates wrinkles or a coupled-up anniversary photo that preceded a furious argument. Remember that you, too, had fun at the weekend – you were just enjoying yourself too much to photograph it.

*See also Online Manners*

## SOUP

Push your soup spoon from the front of the bowl away from you to catch a mouthful. Bring the spoon to your mouth and eat from the side, not with the spoon at a 90-degree angle to your mouth.

Don't suck or slurp. Tilt the bowl away from you in order to get the last few spoonfuls. Put your spoon down while you break off pieces of bread. Leave your spoon in the bowl, not on the side plate, when you have finished.
*See also Table Manners*

## SPAM

If you're on the receiving end of unwanted marketing emails, either click on the 'unsubscribe' link or reply to the sender asking to be removed from the company's mailing list.

Spam can also come in the form of nuisance promotional posts on social media. If a friend is responsible for spam posts, you can usually alter your settings to mute their updates or block them altogether.

Don't be guilty of spamming others, either by forwarding endless chain emails or by taking advantage of your social network to promote your business interests. We're all slaves to our inboxes already, without having to feel guilty about ignoring yet another email.
*See also Email*

SPEECHES

*'It usually takes more than three weeks to prepare
a good impromptu speech.'*
MARK TWAIN

A fear of public speaking is one of the UK's top three phobias, more terrifying for most of us than flying, spiders and rodents.

Thorough preparation can help to ease some of the anxiety you might feel about giving a speech: rehearsal and repetition of your material will have a numbing effect, making you less susceptible to an attack of nerves.

It might sound obvious, but having a clear focus for your speech will make it more arresting. Avoid inappropriate topics by thinking about the purpose of your speech: is it intended to amuse and entertain (after-dinner, wedding, special occasion); is it inspirational (political gathering); or is it intended to exhort (sales conference, etc.)?

Think about your potential audience, too: their frame of reference, sense of humour, age and predominant gender – if you understand your listeners, your jokes, anecdotes and references will not fall on stony ground.

Next, research your topic thoroughly (never be caught out faltering, or uncertain of your facts). Write your speech down and ensure that it is well-paced: do not overload it with dense information, and jokes and anecdotes should be evenly dispersed.

Practise your speech – preferably in front of a mirror or a willing friend – and time exactly how long it takes. Allow time for audience reaction.

When it comes to delivering your speech, look up frequently, maintain eye contact with your audience, speak slowly, and pause if you are expecting a reaction.

If you are dry-mouthed and nervous, don't have any qualms about pausing to take a sip of water. Engage with your audience – you may be the only one speaking, but a good speech will elicit a response from your listeners.
*See also Formal Dinners*

## SPILLAGES AND BREAKAGES

If somebody spills wine on your carpet or sends a precious vase flying at a party, it's your job to remain calm, contain the fall-out and assuage the culprit's guilt.

There are few stains that cannot be removed (there is invariably someone at a party who is an authority on stain removal). Breakages can be more upsetting, but losing your cool won't repair the situation – or the item.

If you are responsible for either calamity, ensure that you offer to help clear the wreckage. Await guidance from the host before weighing in with a napkin or dustpan and brush.

After the clean-up, apologise sincerely and, if appropriate, offer to replace the item or pay for the damage. If you are on the receiving end of the apology, accept it graciously and decline payment.

If nobody witnessed the drama, own up to it. Don't be tempted to cover your tracks: it will be highly embarrassing if you are discovered.

### SPITTING

Never spit in public. Professional sportsmen were once forgiven for spitting on the pitch, but television close-ups have made even this exception off-limits.

### SPOILERS

Inadvertently revealing a crucial plot twist or development from a film or television series is a serious social faux pas in a world addicted to entertainment on-demand.

Before discussing a TV episode or film with anyone, check first that they have seen it to make sure you're not in spoiler territory. Be particularly wary on social media or message groups: even cryptic references and emojis can give information away.

If you do accidentally let slip a spoiler, a profound apology will usually go some way to repairing the damage.

If you're on the receiving end of an accidental spoiler, try to bear it with good humour rather than complaining or getting your revenge with a reciprocal spoiler.

## SPORTSMANSHIP

Despite the antics of professional players the world over, sport isn't just about winning the game, it's about playing well. This means being magnanimous in victory and gracious in defeat.

Sportsmanship is no more than good manners: congratulating your opponents on good play and accepting the decisions of the referee or umpire graciously – no whining, arguing or sulking. If you score a goal or win the match, rein in the celebrations to spare the feelings of the opposition.

As an effective sportsman, you will have a highly developed sense of competition, but as a good sportsman, you will never let competitiveness override good conduct.

## STRESS

Irritability, insomnia, inability to concentrate, smoking, drinking, nail-biting – for many of us, the symptoms of stress are overwhelming and hard to control. But stress is never an excuse for bad manners.

Try to deal with your stress before it takes over, but equally, remember that many problems and anxieties can lessen with some time, sleep and perspective.

Certain activities can help you overcome stress, such as practising mindfulness techniques or meditation, or taking exercise. Try to avoid too much alcohol, get plenty of sleep and eat well.

If you can feel your stress levels rising and you have no recourse to these techniques, go somewhere private where you can release your internal tension in a physical way: by hitting a cushion, for example, or by making angry faces at yourself in the mirror. Then take a deep breath and reinstate your calm and well-mannered persona. Adhering to a code of impeccable manners can give you a feeling of control, often an effective way of easing stress.

## STUBBLE

Although fashionable, stubble runs the risk of looking careless and like you simply haven't had time to shave. In formal working environments, it is usually not appropriate, and it is best avoided if your facial hair doesn't grow evenly.

If you are trying to grow a beard, wait for a long period of near-seclusion to get you through the stubbly halfway house to full bearded plumage: the Christmas break, for example, or a summer holiday.

*See also Beards*

## SUPERMARKETS

Crowded, noisy and confusingly full of choices, supermarkets can be an assault on the senses. Adopt good supermarket manners and you will avoid some of the stress.

Be a considerate trolley-pusher: negotiate your way carefully around obstacles, don't barge into other trolleys, and don't leave your trolley or basket blocking the aisle as you forage on the shelves.

At areas where food is exposed such as the bakery or salad bar, use the implements provided, never your hands, and try to keep it tidy.

At the checkout, unload your shopping on to the conveyor, then place the divider ready for the next shopper. Have your bags and payment ready, and don't text or talk on your phone while the checkout assistant processes your shopping.

*See also Self-checkout; Shopping*


## SURNAMES

While it was always traditional for a bride to adopt her new husband's surname upon marriage, she is not required to do so, and many married women now choose to retain their maiden (unmarried) name. If a woman decides to retain her maiden name, she can adopt her husband's name at any time in the future without a deed poll.

Other women retain their maiden name at work and use their new, married surname in non-professional situations. Increasingly, men are choosing to relinquish their own surnames instead, in favour of their new wife's.

Double-barrelled surnames are also popular, while 'hybrid' surnames (eg. 'Brownstone' if a Brown marries a Stone) are becoming increasingly common. In the case of the latter, each half of the couple needs to change his or her surname by deed poll.

For same-sex marriages, one spouse may choose to adopt the surname of the other, or the couple could combine surnames.

## SUSHI

The preparation and consumption of sushi is highly ritualistic. Understanding the finer points of this may be difficult for Westerners, but some basic principles should be observed.

Miso soup is taken as a starter, and can be drunk straight from the bowl. Soy sauce should be poured into your saucer with wasabi mixed in, if you wish. It is polite to pour your dining companions' sauce too.

Dip sashimi (sliced raw fish on its own) into the sauce with your chopsticks and eat. Sushi rolls and nigiri (blocks of rice with fish on top) should be eaten whole; attempting to bite in two can lead to a scattering of debris across the table. It is not obligatory to use chopsticks when eating sushi, but it is always best to use them in formal company.

When sushi is served in small plates on a conveyor belt, ensure that you only take what you plan to eat. Forming a line of dishes is unnecessary and waste is frowned upon.

*See also Chopsticks*

## SWEARING

The acceptability of certain words has changed over the years, and today the line between a shocking profanity and a harmless exclamation has become blurred.

The Victorian editor Thomas Bowdler 'bowdlerised' various famous works, carefully censoring all sexual allusion and bawdy language (even a 'bull' became a 'gentleman cow').

Now, at the other end of the spectrum, expletives like 'damn' and 'bloody hell' are seamlessly part of the lingo, where once they were the height of rudeness. Everyday speech is infiltrated by swear words, and even the F-word is no longer censored on post-watershed television.

Scientists have shown that swearing emanates from the lower brain, the part that processes emotion and instinct. It does have benefits – it can ease physical pain and reduce stress levels – but swearing should be used with discernment. A conversation peppered with expletives is one where both meaning and language is being diluted. How can you expect someone to respect what you are saying if

you are distracting them with swear words?

Suppressing, or at the very least controlling, your worst language will have many benefits: you won't cause offence to others, you will be a better example to your children, and you may even dream up some more linguistically creative ways of expressing rage. Be aware of your swearing and keep your worst insults for life's most challenging situations — if every sentence is peppered with obscenities, what will happen when you need to be truly insulting?

TABLE MANNERS TO
TRUSTWORTHINESS

## TABLE MANNERS

Dining politely should be second nature – or should at least appear to be. We all indulge in less-than perfect behaviour in private, or in very familiar company, but some consistency at home and away will help you avoid the more serious table offences.

The number one dining crime is eating noisily. Keeping your mouth closed while chewing and taking care not to overfill it will enable you to breathe steadily.

Eat at a relaxed pace and really think about your food. Not only does this make you appreciate what's on your plate, but it can also help you moderate your intake. Inhaling course after course not only looks greedy, but doesn't give you time to realise you're full.

This is particularly important when dining with just one other person; your date will feel exposed if you wolf your food and attempt full-on conversation while he or she is still eating.

Avoid talking while there is food in your mouth – even when you have a conversational gem up your sleeve. Try to avoid directing a question at someone who is mid-mouthful, but don't despair if you mistime. A smile and an understanding nod will encourage them to swallow without rushing, spluttering or making sheepish gestures.

When dining in a group, always put others' needs before your own. Do your bit in offering communal dishes around the table, and hold them to assist your neighbour. If you are served a meal that is already on the plate, wait until everyone has been served before picking up your cutlery.

Napkins should be placed on your lap — never tucked into the front of your shirt. Never gesture with your cutlery, and keep the tines of your fork facing downwards — unless it is your sole eating implement, in which case using it scoop-style is acceptable.

When you have finished, place your knife and fork — with the tines facing upwards — together on your plate.

If you are served a dish that is not to your taste, try to soldier on to avoid hurt feelings. If you can't finish your meal, apologise to your host and explain that your appetite has failed you.

Always attempt to sparkle conversationally, and don't monopolise one neighbour to the exclusion of another.

Don't forget to compliment the cook.

*See also Cutlery; Food, Photographing; Napkins; Soup*


## TABLE SETTINGS

The range of cutlery provided will depend on the formality of the occasion, but the layout will usually be forks to the left, knives and spoons to the right, and pudding implements above the place setting. A knife for buttering bread may be placed on or near the side plate, and to the left of the place setting. Simply work from the outside into the middle.

Glasses should be placed to the right of the setting, and different glasses should be provided for red wine, white wine, water and, if you are serving it, champagne.

Napkins can be folded simply; there is no need for elaborate swans or fans. Name cards are not necessary at casual gatherings, but it is the host's decision to seat guests where he or she thinks appropriate. Ensure that table decorations don't inhibit eye contact or conversation.
*See also Cutlery*

## TABOO TOPICS

Few conversation topics are completely off the table nowadays, but when you don't know people well, it is advisable to avoid certain subjects – such as death, disease or religion – for fear of causing upset or offence.

Certain questions are also considered presumptuous in the UK: enquiries after age, weight, salary or marital status are best avoided.

Remember that conversational taboos also depend to a large extent on culture and religion. If you are travelling abroad, take your cue from others and read up beforehand on topics that are best avoided.

As you get to know people better, you will feel able to stray into more challenging territory, but always do so with caution. Some people are very private, and may well want to avoid discussing more intimate subjects.

## TACT

*'Talk to every woman as if you loved her, and to every man as if he loved you and … you will have the reputation of possessing the most perfect social tact.'*
OSCAR WILDE

Tact is the skill of handling a delicate situation and emerging with everyone still smiling. It is the ability to steer the staunch socialist away from the right-wing reactionary without either of them even knowing the other one was there. Those of us who come back from every party wracked with guilt about what we said, did, or looked like when we danced, long to possess tact.

There is a hint of dishonesty in tact, but a little dash of duplicity is surely acceptable if it's to spare someone else's feelings. It is an unselfish art, where the tactful one removes himself or herself from the context to think only about others.

By contrast, there is something selfish and thoughtless about being tactless: at best, an inability to avoid putting one's foot in it — at a cost to other people's feelings or sensibilities — or, at worst, a wilful ignorance about the effect your own words can have on others. 'A tactless man is like an axe on an embroidery frame', says an old Malay proverb — how much better to be the one who stitches a situation back together again.

## TAXIS

Whether you request a nearby taxi via an app or book a minicar in advance of your journey, try not to keep your driver waiting once he or she arrives.

Resist the urge to micro-manage the route: most taxi services now use GPS to determine the quickest way to your destination.

Keep the taxi tidy and be polite to your driver. Thank him or her when they drop you off at your destination and don't slam the door when you get out.

Many taxi apps now include the option to tip your driver, and will usually suggest an amount. It is fair to add a tip to your fare if you have had a positive experience. Similarly, leave your driver a good review if appropriate.

If you are hailing a taxi from the street, wait until you see one with its light on, i.e. available for hire, then lift your arm and lean out from the pavement to get the driver's attention. Tell the driver your destination before getting in. At your destination, get out and pay the driver through the front window. The going rate for tipping is ten per cent.

*See also Tipping*


## TEA

It is worth brewing a pot if you are serving tea for a group, and a second pot of hot water should be provided to dilute over-brewed tea if necessary. If a waiter places a teapot on the table without pouring the tea, the person nearest the pot should pour for everyone.

Milk or a slice of lemon and sugar should be added after the tea has been poured. If the teapot contains loose tea, pour through a tea strainer. After stirring, remove the spoon from the cup and place it on the saucer.

Hold the handle of the teacup between your thumb and forefinger; don't hold your little finger in the air. Don't dunk biscuits in your tea unless in an informal setting, and don't slurp — even if it is piping hot.

## TEASING

There is a fine line, when teasing, between that which is affectionate and amusing and that which is destructive and unfunny. Teasing is a great way of showing your wit and cutting someone else down to size in a non-aggressive way — but for both, there are crucial parameters.

The rule of thumb should be calibrated by how much the other person can take. If they are fabulously confident, popular and successful, they can — and should — take some teasing. If they are diffident or shy, be gentle, and only tease when you know them well.

Teasing is often most rife within a family, but there are limits. Broadly speaking, family teasing should acknowledge the quirks that make someone loved, not the traits that irritate everyone around them.

When being teased yourself, it is hard to remain calm and good-humoured, but you must. Your reaction to teasing will leave a longer-lasting impression than whatever it is you are being teased about. Better still is the ability to disarm teasers with some related self-deprecation of your own, rather than becoming defensive or retaliatory.

Above all, don't take teasing too seriously: remember that it's intended more for others' benefit than as a genuine lesson for you.

*See also Humour; Jokes*

## TEENAGERS

The teenage years are notoriously challenging for both children and their parents. While teenagers' hormones are raging, their bodies changing, and their need for independence asserting itself, parents have to reconcile themselves to the fact that their adorable angel has morphed into an uncommunicative phone addict who flinches at the sight of daylight.

Try to connect with teenagers on their own level: learn to use their favourite apps to communicate, but don't embarrass them with public declarations of affection or by posting compromising photographs on social media. However charming their friends seem by comparison, don't assume you can befriend them: your own child is probably equally pleasant to his or her friends' parents.

The worst crime you can commit as the parent of a teenager is to show your face at a teenage party or gathering. If you've offered to give your child a lift, remain in the car as instructed — even if it makes you feel like a chauffeur — and bombard them with phone calls and text messages until they emerge.

On the other hand, the threat of causing embarrassment remains your one weapon — and should be used judiciously.

However disconcerted you are by this new phase in your child's life, accept that normal teenagers are just differently mannered and consider it a challenge to your diplomacy and negotiating skills.

Hail their occasional appearance during daytime hours with good grace, welcome every grunt as if it were a pearl of pure wisdom, and use humour to chip away at their uncooperative defences.

## TEXT MESSAGES

Text messages are quick and convenient, but shouldn't be used to communicate important information or anything that needs a lengthy explanation. If you have to cancel an appointment, always make a phone call; apologies will be better received this way.

Handwritten thank you letters are preferable to text messages; nor should you ever end a relationship by text.

There's no need to use confusing, abbreviated text

language. Use as much conventional grammar, spelling and punctuation as possible to make yourself understood. The usual salutations and sign-offs can be ignored.

Don't send or read text messages when you are driving, out in company or being served in a restaurant or shop. Turn your phone to silent when in a meeting or a 'quiet zone' on a train.

*See also Message Groups; Mobile Phones*

## THANK YOU NOTES / LETTERS

Taking the time to write when you have received a present, hospitality or some other kindness, reassures the giver that their efforts are appreciated.

A handwritten letter or card is preferable to an email or text message, but digital thanks are better than none. Talk around the subject — why you loved that particular present or what you most enjoyed about your visit.

On those occasions when you are likely to receive a number of presents (a wedding or the arrival of a baby, for example), make a note of who gave what and try to commit it to memory. Parents should write thank you letters on behalf of their children until the children are old enough to do so, when they should be encouraged to write themselves.

Letters or cards should be sent as promptly as possible, but when it comes to saying thank you, late is invariably better than never.

## TIPPING

The practice of tipping varies from country to country, so before travelling, it is worth consulting a guide book to ensure that you are familiar with the custom and do not cause offence.

As of 2018 in the UK, a 12.5% service charge is usually added to restaurant bills automatically, but you may wish to check that your waiter or waitress receives the tip rather than the management: if not, ask that this charge is removed and leave a separate cash tip. Similarly, if service has been noticeably poor, you are not obliged to leave a tip or pay a service charge.

Tipping is also commonplace in hair and beauty salons and in hotels. Use discretion, but err on the side of generosity.

*See also Hotels, Restaurants; Taxis*

## TITLES

People with titles do not necessarily use them in every situation, but it is safer to opt for formality, particularly when dealing with the older generation. It may require some research to ensure you get a title correct: consult the *Debrett's Handbook* or website, or ask the individual what style of address they prefer.

In correspondence, use the full title on envelopes. When introducing those with titles or referring to them in conversation, a general guide is to use Lord and Lady in the same way as you would use Mr and Mrs. Do not use their descriptive title such as 'the Earl of Lonsdale' or 'the Marquess of Bristol.' The only exceptions are dukes and duchesses who are spoken to and referred to as the Duke and Duchess of Marlborough, for example, and addressed, in writing, as Duke and Duchess.

*See also Debrett's Handbook*

## TOLERANCE

*'Tolerance implies no lack of commitment to one's own beliefs. Rather it condemns the oppression or persecution of others.'*
JOHN F KENNEDY

Tolerance is at the heart of modern manners. George Eliot wrote, 'The responsibility of tolerance lies with those who have the wider vision', and there remains a need for that wider vision or education to be the seedbed of tolerance. You can't expect a toddler to be tolerant of someone taking his toys – he hasn't learned the implications of sharing being a two-way street.

If faced with a lack of tolerance in someone else, think of them as acting like that toddler. That's not to say that one should tolerate intolerance silently (though in some circumstances it might be better to swallow what you were going to say and simply move on), but if you can persuade yourself that the intolerant one does not know what they are saying, it could make the conversation more peaceful and polite.

Finally, tolerance does not imply weakness, so if it means turning the other cheek, do so knowing that you are acting from a position of strength.

## TRAINS

*'Railway termini are our gates to the glorious and the unknown.
Through them we pass out into adventure and sunshine,
to them, alas! we return.'*
E. M. FORSTER

The slings and arrows suffered by the British train traveller are legendary: delays, overcrowding, cancellations, and trains that mysteriously divide en route, transporting you to Penzance when you were trying to get to Tunbridge Wells.

Basic good manners and respect for your fellow passengers will go some way towards making even the most packed train journeys more tolerable.

Wait for other passengers to exit before boarding the train, rather than trying to shove past people as they are trying to get off. Always give up your seat to someone who is elderly, disabled or obviously pregnant. Mothers with small children should also be given priority.

If necessary, help people to put their luggage in the overhead racks. Some train carriages are very quiet, packed with commuters reading newspapers or working on their laptops, so be aware that loud phone conversations are very disturbing.

If you are going to listen to music, ensure that you have soundproof headphones. Be aware that other passengers may not appreciate you eating greasy, smelly food like a burger or kebab.

If the carriage is crowded, don't take up an additional seat with your excess baggage, and don't sprawl in your seat, spread your legs too wide, or put dirty feet on the seat opposite. Help people off the train with heavy baggage, and dispose of any rubbish – no one will want to sit surrounded by your detritus.

*See also Public Transport; Quiet Zones*

## TRAVEL BORES

*'The World is a book, and those who do not travel read only a page.'*
SAINT AUGUSTINE

Travel bores are one of the unfortunate side-effects of the travel revolution – where once, the tales of derring-do abroad could thrill for hours, now we are inundated daily with photographs of deserted beaches, ruined temples and sedated tigers.

A travel bore is not difficult to recognise: soon they'll be regaling you with dysentery anecdotes and recommending hostels on the Khao San Road.

If you are brimming with your own travel anecdotes, mind that what you say is not just a rehash of what others have said before you. Try to gauge the attention span of your listeners and be aware that your audience may not be as hungry for new experiences as you think they should be.

Don't overestimate the lasting effect of your travels. No matter how many life-changing experiences you might have had, it's unlikely that they will change you permanently as a person. Soon you'll find yourself grumbling in a queue for your morning latte again, like everyone else.

*See also Bores, Escaping From*


## TRUSTWORTHINESS

*'A man who trusts nobody is apt to be the kind of man nobody trusts.'*
HAROLD MACMILLAN

You will acquire a reputation as a reliable and trustworthy person if you follow these rules: do what you say you're going to do, never promise more than you can deliver, arrive on time, be honest in all your financial dealings, and never reveal other people's secrets. Above all, never betray another person's trust.

*See also Secrets*

UNDERDRESSED TO
UXORIOUSNESS

## UNDERDRESSED

There are few things less comfortable than feeling underdressed for an occasion. It is always best to err on the side of formality; if you find you are overdressed, a tie or jacket can be easily discarded, and heels swapped for flats. It is much harder to dress up a casual look, especially if you don't know the hosts well enough to borrow items of clothing. If you are unsure about the formality of an event, or worried about the dress code, check with the host beforehand. It is better to look over-anxious than underdressed.

*See also Smart Casual*

## UNDERSTATEMENT

A quality valued by the British, understatement permeates our humour and is frequently seen as being synonymous with good manners.

Understatement is characterised by negatives: a refusal to be effusive or emphatic. Remarks are frequently accompanied by tentative or provisional qualifications: 'perhaps', 'I wonder if', or 'maybe'. The overall effect is an aura of modest reticence, quiet understanding and considerate behaviour. Like self-deprecation, understatement is an attractive and effective quality, which is often more persuasive, and appealing, than a direct approach.

Take care that your use of understatement doesn't mean you are misunderstood. Saying that a piece of work is 'not bad at all', when you mean that it's really very good, won't always convey the requisite level of enthusiasm to the colleague you are praising.

Similarly, telling a plumber that you've got a 'bit of an issue' with your toilet cistern may not express sufficient urgency if the bathroom has flooded and the ceiling is threatening to cave in.

*See also Ostentation*

## URINALS

Always leave an empty urinal between you and the next man; if this is not possible, use the cubicle. Look straight ahead. Don't talk. Don't make eye contact.

## UXORIOUSNESS

*'Uxoriousness, n. A perverted affection that has strayed to one's own wife.'*
AMBROSE BIERCE

A man who dotes on his wife (or a woman on her husband, for that matter) is to be applauded, but there is a point at which such marital dedication can tip into the realm of bad manners. Happily married couples should be aware that their devotion to each other can make others feel excluded.

As two very lucky people, who are happy to be with each other, it is your responsibility to make people around you comfortable. This means taking the focus away from each other and turning your attention towards other people: no kissing, pet names or giggling at private jokes. You will have plenty of time, and privacy, in which to enjoy each other's company – just try to ensure that other people enjoy being with you.

*See also Affection, Public Displays of*

VALENTINE'S DAY
TO VOICEMAIL

## VALENTINE'S DAY

Valentine's Day is an opportunity for the romantically inclined to celebrate love and relationships. It is wise to be relaxed about the whole thing, but take your cue from your beloved. Be wary of those who noisily deride Valentine's Day, only to be furious when they find themselves present-less and card-less come the big day.

Some venues insist on offering themed menus, but unless your Valentine expects it, restaurants are generally best avoided – the pressure can be stifling. If you are in the business of gift-giving, either be prepared to spend serious cash on beautiful flowers, or opt for something more imaginative. A thoughtless offering is worse than nothing at all.

For the unattached, anonymous cards have their own pitfalls: you run the risk of being seen as either too feeble to come forward in person or, worse, as a stalker. Unless you are an incurable romantic – and a patient one at that – there is no need to wait for Valentine's Day to reveal your feelings for someone.

## VAPING

Almost 3 million people in the UK now vape, a practice that satisfies a craving for nicotine while eliminating some of the harmful elements of tobacco.

The long-term health implications of vaping are yet to be fully established, but public bodies are increasingly

recognising its effectiveness as a way of quitting smoking.

Early incarnations of e-cigarettes tended to mimic cigarettes in look and size, but are now often larger and more noticeable, with a mouthpiece and a cartridge containing a flavoured juice. They may make a low bubbling noise as the user inhales, and tend to emit larger clouds of vapour on exhalation.

The social rules around vaping are still being established, and many workplaces and public places such as bars and restaurants have their own vaping policies, so ask first if you're not sure whether or not it's acceptable to vape.

Bear in mind that some elements of vaping can still distract and irritate others — whether it's the noise, the large clouds of vapour, or the smell — however sweet and appealing it smells to you.

Vapers should not be lumped together automatically with smokers: if they are using e-cigarettes as a way of weaning themselves off smoking, it's unfair to make them use designated smoking areas at work or in public places, so if you manage a business or lead a team of people, try to find alternative spaces in which to accommodate vapers.

## VEGANS

The popularity of veganism has soared in recent years, with campaigns like Veganuary encouraging carnivores to moderate their dependency on meat.

Abstaining from all animal by-products – dairy and eggs as well as meat – vegans are more awkward to cater for than vegetarians, but many supermarkets now offer vegan substitutes and there are countless simple recipes available online, so make the effort if you are hosting a vegan for a meal.

The unkind characterisation of vegans as holier-than-thou mouthpieces for their cause is less prevalent nowadays, but if you are vegan – whether for ethical or health reasons – resist the urge to take the moral high ground or to convert others with too much zeal: if the current trend continues, pretty soon you won't have to.

## VEGETARIANS

Compared with veganism, clean eating and raw foodism, vegetarianism looks increasingly moderate as modern lifestyle choices go.

If you're a vegetarian and invited to a dinner party, you should still let your host know beforehand to avoid potential embarrassment. Likewise, a host should accommodate a vegetarian when planning their menu – and not just by allocating them extra side vegetables.

## VIDEO CALLS

Whether you are speaking to family on the other side of the country or to colleagues overseas, video calls can be

chaotic and counterproductive, leaving callers too distracted by the miracle of technology to listen to what the other person is saying.

Don't feel you have to shout: the other people on the call should be able to hear you as long as you are speaking near a microphone. Unless you are speaking to a child, there's no need to wave or mime to make yourself understood.

Don't be distracted by the image of yourself in miniature in the corner, and resist the urge to groom or preen if you spot a hair out of place.

If you are delivering a presentation over a shared-screen video call, be aware that the people to whom you are presenting may still be able to see you, so continue as if you were meeting in person and avoid fidgeting, picking your nose or staring vacuously out of the window.

For an interview or work video call from home, be sure to dress appropriately, at least as far as is visible — even if that means wearing business attire on the top half of your body and pyjamas on the bottom.

## VISITORS, UNEXPECTED

*'Santa Claus has the right idea. Visit people once a year.'*
VICTOR BORGE

While it is the height of good manners to be hospitable under all circumstances, it is also the height of bad manners to turn up unannounced and expect someone to be hospitable towards you when they've had no warning.

So how do you treat the unexpected visitor? How much onus is on you, the reluctant but impeccably mannered host? Friends who've popped in for a surprise cup of tea should be welcomed warmly if you have time for their visit, but it is fine to tell them straight if you're too busy to spend more than a few minutes with them.

Staying guests require equally firm handling because they have broken the unspoken rule that says you let someone know when you're coming to see them. They should be happy to get clean sheets, a roof over their head and instructions as to what is available to eat in the fridge and cupboards.

Having turned up unexpectedly, the visitor should not then compound their faux pas by outstaying their welcome, and even if you are welcomed with open arms, don't make the mistake of repeating your gaffe.

*See also Guests, House*

## VOICEMAIL

As mobile phones increasingly replace landlines, so too is voicemail fading from use. A missed call notification is usually sufficient to let the other person know that you have tried to contact them and would like them to return your call.

VOICEMAIL

If you do use a voicemail service, personalise the message so that people know they have got through to the correct person.

If you are leaving a message on somebody else's voicemail, don't ramble; be concise and leave your name and a contact number.

*See also Mobile Phones*

WASTEFUL, BEING
TO WINE

## WASTEFUL, BEING

Bewildering levels of choice, combined with over-cautious
expiry dates and plus-size portions, all make it difficult
not to end up throwing away much of what we purchase.

It is worth identifying where you are being wasteful
and making changes to shopping habits and energy use to
ensure that your consumption is proportionate. Switch
off lights in empty rooms, only use as much water as you
need, and look online for imaginative recipes to revive
limp salad leaves and sprouting potatoes.

## WEATHER, TALKING ABOUT

*'It is commonly observed, that when two Englishmen meet,
their first talk is of the weather.'*
SAMUEL JOHNSON

English people are notorious for their endless
fascination with the weather, a topic that is deployed
nationwide as an ice-breaker.

The primary function of this fascination with the
weather is, of course, to break down the English person's
natural reserve; it offers a universal, and neutral, topic,
which everyone, from a small child to an elderly
grandmother, enjoys discussing.

Other countries endure far more noteworthy weather
events — droughts, hurricanes, tornadoes — but British
weather is, above all, unpredictable. Sunshine, showers,
wind and snow sweep across the country with extraordi-

nary rapidity, providing an ever-changing outlook, meaning that with the weather as a topic, conversation is never going to falter.

*See also Conversation*

## WEDDING LISTS

The circumstances and age of the bride and groom often influence the choice of wedding list and presents. A young couple setting up home will have different priorities from an older, established couple who already live together.

Lists are available through department stores, specialist wedding list companies, independent shops or charities.

Guests are able to buy online, in-store or over the phone. It is becoming increasingly common to ask for a financial contribution or vouchers towards the cost of a honeymoon, although couples should be aware that some guests may not feel comfortable giving cash. Most couples include details of the wedding list with the invitations.

Guests should not think that they are being unoriginal by buying from the list — the couple has specifically requested those items. However, a guest is free to do something different if they would like to give a unique or individual present.

It is a gracious gesture for guests who are unable to attend a wedding to give a present.

*See also Presents*

## WEDDINGS, ATTENDING

Weddings are special occasions and guests should feel privileged that they have been invited. The wishes of the bride and groom should be respected – it is, after all, their day – and guests should try to be flexible and fit in with plans.

Book any accommodation well in advance; the host will usually recommend somewhere local or have secured a block-booking. Remember to check whether there is any transport laid on, or if you need to book a taxi.

Presents are either bought in advance from the couple's list, or you may prefer to take something along on the day. There is usually an area at the reception for guests to leave presents – make sure your gift is clearly labelled.

Guests should be appropriately dressed. Dress codes are not included on a wedding invitation unless the couple is opting for something unusual (such as black tie). It is, however, traditional for men to wear morning dress, or a suit with a shirt and tie.

Women may wear a suit, skirt and blouse or a dress – appropriate for the season and the weather – and may also wear a hat or fascinator. Head-to-toe outfits in white or cream should never be worn and all black, unless cleverly accessorised, may look too sombre.

Wedding guests should familiarise themselves with the order of the day. Be punctual for the ceremony and help the ushers by telling them if you are a guest of the bride or groom (or both), friend or family.

Weddings are usually a long day, with unusual meal times and many celebratory drinks and toasts. Pace yourself to ensure you last the course.

*See also Hats*

## WEIGHT, DISCUSSING

Few of us are the weight we would ideally like to be (or that society would like us to be), and discussing weight takes up almost as much airtime as the weather, with slimming organisations, low-calorie cookery books and celebrity exercise DVDs fuelling the conversation. There is no longer anything sacred or private about the subject of one's shape.

The accepted code of conduct is as follows: any discussion of your own weight is tedious but acceptable – unless you are being boastful. Any discussion of another person's weight is still beyond the pale. Never feel so liberated by your freedom in discussing your own weight that you think you have carte blanche to introduce someone else to the party. Comments along the lines of, 'I've found this amazing diet, perhaps you should try it?' are never going to be welcomed, no matter how flabby the focus of your question.

Commenting on someone's weight loss can be just as risky: a brief general compliment on their appearance – such as 'you look great!' – is preferable to dwelling on

the astonishing number of pounds they have shed.
However staggering the transformation, no one wants to
believe that you previously considered them a colossus.
*See also Diets; Hunger*


## WHINING

*'It takes a genius to whine appealingly.'*
F. SCOTT FITZGERALD

Also known as whingeing, whining is an abomination,
and rarely works. Even if, by sheer persistence, your
whining beats your target down until they agree to
everything, it's a hollow victory. They have either lost the
will to live, or they will resent you for forcing them to do
something they don't want to do.

To some people – usually parents of small children
– whining becomes like wallpaper; it's always there in
the background but they no longer notice it. But others
surely do – and to them it is the height of offensive
noise pollution.

Nowadays we have more power to whine effectively by
doing so on a public platform – whether it's warning the
world not to use the trainline that made us late for a
meeting, or by complaining that the council has yet again
neglected to empty the bins. Play fair, and complain
directly to those responsible in the first instance before
resorting to open warfare.

### WHISKY / WHISKEY

If you've ever wondered which is the correct spelling, whiskey with an 'e' is produced in Ireland or in the USA, while everywhere else forgoes the extra letter.

A blended whisky is composed of a blend of single grain and single malt whiskies that have been distilled at more than one distillery.

Single malts are produced from malted barley at a single distillery. They vary considerably in character and appreciating them can become a life's work. Bourbon is made in the USA, primarily from corn, and is distilled in oak casks.

Whisky should be drunk however you like it best; it is no longer frowned upon to add water or ice to a single malt, and blended whisky might be mixed with soft drinks such as lemonade or ginger ale. Whisky is best drunk from a heavy-based crystal glass to concentrate the aroma.

### WHISPERING

*'Alas! they had been friends in youth; but whispering tongues can poison truth.'*
SAMUEL TAYLOR COLERIDGE

Whispering is a crude weapon of social rejection; by advertising intimacy with one person, you are also excluding everyone else. Whispering inevitably induces paranoia in the people around you, and at the very least makes them feel uncomfortable. In a group situation, remember your school days, and don't whisper something to one person that you don't feel comfortable conveying to the whole group. If you want to share a secret, save it for later.

Whispering to your companion when you're at the cinema, theatre or a concert, is inconsiderate to the people around you. No matter how quietly you think you're talking, your whispering will be both audible and distracting.

*See also Gossip; Secrets*


## WHISTLING

If you're prone to whistling, be aware that you may be doing it unconsciously. People will be very irritated if they are forced to listen to your musical renditions in quiet areas – trains, museums, offices and so on.

Whistling is done for the whistler's enjoyment, and as such, indulging in private is the safest course of action.

Whistling loudly through your fingers is only appropriate to capture attention on the sports pitch or to signal approval during a round of applause at a concert or show.

## WHITE TIE

*'With an evening coat ... anyone, even a stockbroker,
can gain a reputation for being civilised.'*
OSCAR WILDE

White tie — also referred to as 'full evening dress' — is the
most formal, and rare, of dress codes, worn in the
evening for royal ceremonies and balls. It may also be
specified for formal evening weddings.

For men, traditional white tie consists of:

- A black single-breasted tail coat with silk lapels,
  worn unbuttoned (never to be confused with a
  morning coat).
- Black trousers to match the tail coat, with two lines of
  braid down each outside leg.
- A white marcella shirt, worn with a detachable wing
  collar, cufflinks and studs.
- A thin, white, hand-tied marcella bow-tie.
- A white marcella evening waistcoat — double- or
  single-breasted.
- Black patent lace-up shoes and black silk socks.

In winter, a black overcoat and white silk scarf can be
worn. It is rare nowadays to wear a top hat and many see it
as unnecessary as it is only worn en route to the event,
and therefore generally goes unnoticed.

For women, white tie usually means a full-length,
formal evening dress or skirt. Jewellery can be striking and
may include tiaras. Traditionally these are worn for the

first time by brides, and subsequently by married women only. It is not customary for young girls to wear tiaras.
*See also Black Tie*

## WIND
Blame the dog, even if there isn't one.

## WINE
*'Let us have wine and women, mirth and laughter,*
*Sermons and soda-water the day after.'*
LORD BYRON

The original social lubricant, wine has the ability to fascinate and delight, perplex and terrify. This is partly because the world of wine boasts infinite variety, but it's also because wine is a social drink that appears shrouded in mystery to the uninitiated.

Fortunately, there are few serious gaffes that you can commit when confronted with a wine list. Many restaurants provide descriptions and suggested food pairings, and if a restaurant is clued-up enough to offer an extensive list, the chances are that there will be someone on hand to advise you on an appropriate choice. Asking for advice is always better than pretending you know more than you do, and it shows that you are interested rather than opting for the same safe bet every time.

If you're responsible for choosing wine for a group, find out what others prefer and what they will be eating before attempting to order a complementary wine. Ordering by the glass can solve the problem of diverging tastes or meal choices, but it's less convivial and more expensive.

If you ordered, you will usually be asked to taste the wine. The waiter will show you the bottle and the cork so that you can verify your wine's identity. You will then be served a very small amount in your glass. This is not your opportunity to decide whether you like the wine; you're simply checking that it's fit to drink. If it's not, you will know immediately. It should smell clean — the merest hint of sherry or a musty aroma indicates a problem.

If the wine smells fine, take a small sip. There is no need for conspicuous sniffing, swirling and gargling. Once you have indicated your approval, everyone else will be served.

There is no shame in buying a screw-cap bottle of wine. The humble twisty cap eliminates the risk of corking, and many well-regarded wine manufacturers are now using it, particularly for wines that are intended for early drinking.

Restaurants vary in their approach to topping up glasses. It is usual for the waiter to keep an eye on supplies, but if they don't, attend to it yourself, unless someone has indicated that they don't want any more. It is usually correct to fill the wine to the widest point

of the glass, but it is better to pour someone too little than too much.

Dealing with wine outside a restaurant is usually less fraught. It is fine to take wine along to a dinner party as a gift, but don't expect it to be opened on the night: your host may have planned which wines to serve with dinner.

If you drink wine, keep a decent bottle in the fridge at home for unexpected visitors or impromptu celebrations.

X-RATED

## X-RATED

Different people will have different parameters for what constitutes acceptable viewing, reading and conversational material. If you meet someone for the first time, err on the side of caution and stick to safe, inoffensive topics while you get the measure of their scandal barometer.

Don't denounce someone as a prude if they were shocked by the language used in your favourite movie: just tailor any future film recommendations towards the 'PG' end of the ratings. Similarly, remember that just because someone has a taste for violence on-screen, doesn't mean they will be vying for a punch-up on a night out.

Much of what we deem acceptable is learnt from a young age, so remember that children are liable to absorb and mimic. Before absent-mindedly swearing in front of your toddler, be aware that he or she may well repeat that colourful expletive at nursery the next day.

The internet now gives almost unlimited access to previously X-rated material. If you are concerned about your children stumbling across unsuitable images or videos while browsing online, find out how you can set parental controls to restrict their access to particular sites.

YAWNING
TO YOGA

## YAWNING

*'Life is too short, and the time we waste in yawning
never can be regained.'*
STENDHAL

Try to refrain from yawning; if you must do so, cover
your mouth with your hand and apologise. Don't inflict
your fatigue on other people — if you're too tired to
socialise without yawning, you should be in bed.

It is even more offensive to yawn out of boredom.
If you're reduced to a state of eye-watering tedium,
make your excuses and leave before your host starts to
take it personally.

## YOGA

Practising yoga requires calm, so don't burst into the
class late and flustered. Instead, slip in silently at the
back or, if over ten minutes late, give it up.

Switch off your phone, don't chat during the class,
and don't groan or protest with each new position. If the
poses really are too hard, try your best to get as near as
possible to what is expected. Respect the aura at all times.

ZEBRA CROSSINGS
TO ZZZZZ

## ZEBRA CROSSINGS

Drivers should slow down at a zebra crossing and check
for pedestrians who are waiting or approaching. Wait
until they have crossed the road before you move away;
never rev your engine as people are crossing. If you can't
treat zebra crossings with patience and courtesy, think of
the alternative – yet another set of traffic lights.

*See also Driving; Road Rage*

## ZIPS

If you notice someone has their flies undone, weigh up
the situation and embark on the path of minimal
embarrassment. If their shirt (or worse) is on display,
the chances are that others will notice. Whatever your
approach, discretion is critical.

If you are on friendly terms, take them to one side and
gently let them know. If, on the other hand, you are
hoping that they will become a business associate, it may
be wise to keep your lips sealed and your eyes firmly
above belt level.

However, there are no hard and fast rules, and you
should rely on your judgement. If someone draws your
attention to your own zip, trust that they have your best
interests at heart, smile confidentially and thank them
for saving you any further embarrassment.

ZZZZZ

## ZZZZZ

Consistently not getting enough sleep can have a serious impact on health: it has been linked to conditions such as obesity, heart disease and diabetes, and has even been shown to shorten life expectancy. In the more immediate term, being over-tired can make you irritable, short-tempered and liable to misjudge situations.

Busy work, social and family lives can make it challenging to get an early night, but you can help yourself by keeping electronic distractions such as phones and laptops away from the bedroom and ensuring your sleeping environment is cool, dark and comfortable.

*See also Awake, Staying*